CHILDREN'S PHOTOGRAPHIC REFERENCE

WORLD ATLAS

This edition published by Parragon Books Ltd in 2013

Parragon Books Ltd
Chartist House
15–17 Trim Street
Bath BA1 1HA, UK
www.parragon.com

ISBN 978-1-4723-2440-5

Printed in Hong Kong

CHILDREN'S PHOTOGRAPHIC REFERENCE
WORLD ATLAS

PaRragon

Bath · New York · Singapore · Hong Kong · Cologne · Delhi
Melbourne · Amsterdam · Johannesburg · Shenzhen

CONTENTS

CENTRAL AMERICA AND THE CARIBBEAN

SOUTH AMERICA

EUROPE

THE AMERICAS

ASIA

OCEANIA

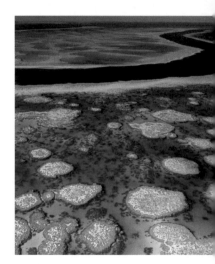

AFRICA

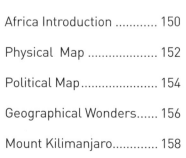

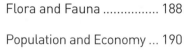

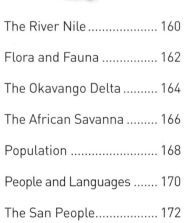

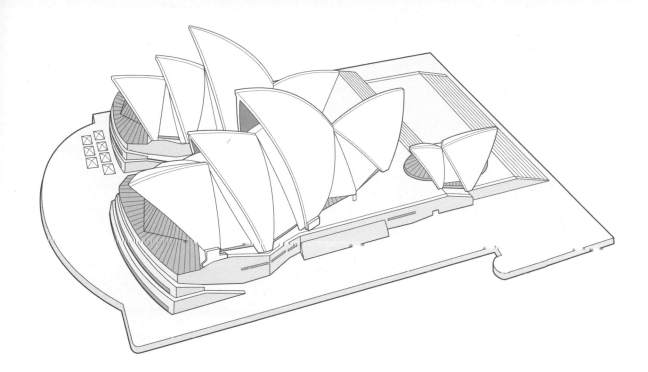

THE WORLD IN FIGURES

The World in Figures

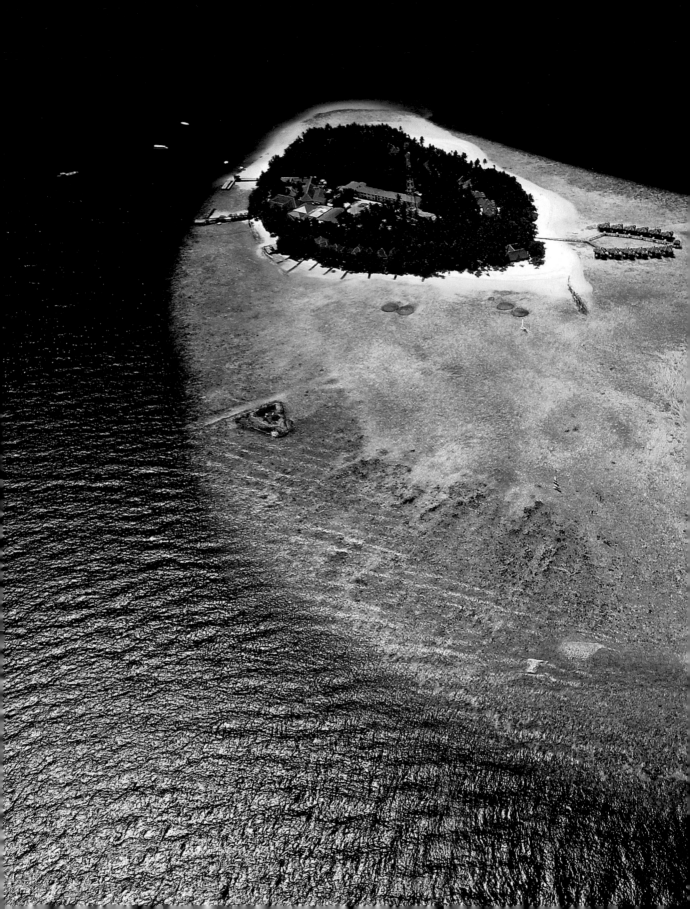

INTRODUCTION

Our planet is an amazing place!

Its seas and oceans are full of incredible plants and animals, from tiny coral to enormous whales.

On land, the scenery ranges from scorching deserts and fertile plains to soaring mountains. These fantastic features have been formed over millions of years by the powerful forces of plate tectonics and the continual action of wind, rain, ice, snow and heat.

This book will take you on an amazing journey through the continents, showing the natural features found in each of them. It will also reveal who lives there and some of the wonderful sites created by humankind.

TROPICAL PARADISE
THIS CORAL ATOLL, SURROUNDED BY A SHALLOW LAGOON, SHOWS ONE
OF THE CHAIN OF 1300 SMALL ISLANDS THAT MAKE UP THE MALDIVES.

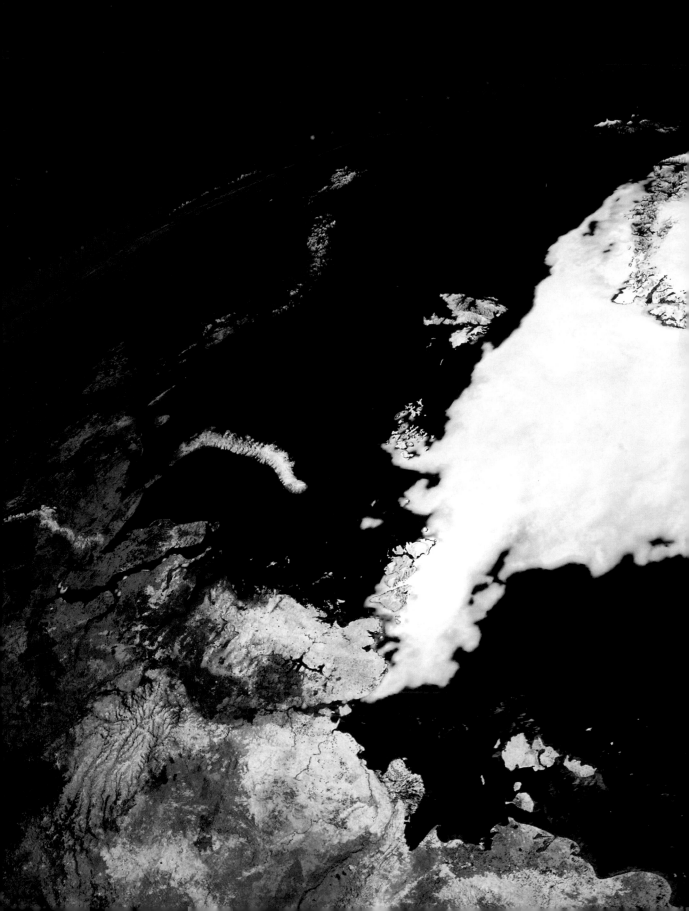

THE WORLD
INTRODUCTION

The Earth is a unique place in our solar system. It is the only planet we know of where life exists. Its surface is teeming with plants and creatures who live in a wide range of habitats. Also living on this planet are more than 7 billion people, who are packed into busy cities or rural settlements.

Deep beneath the Earth's surface, powerful forces push and pull on the thin crust above. These forces can split the land apart causing powerful earthquakes and volcanic eruptions. At the same time, they can send landmasses crashing into each other and push mountains high into the air.

A THICK ICE SHEET
GREENLAND IS COVERED BY A THICK ICE SHEET IN THIS IMAGE TAKEN BY
A SATELLITE IN ORBIT HIGH ABOVE THE EARTH.

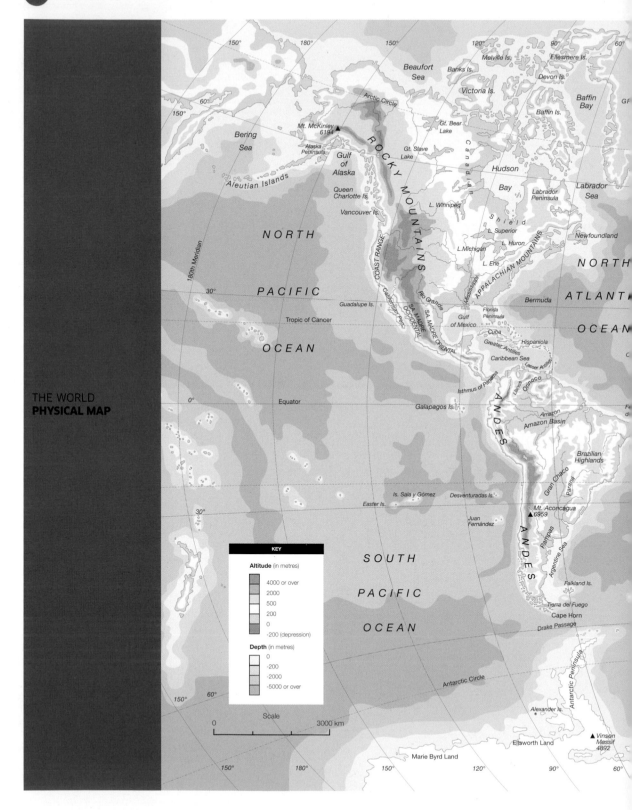

THE WORLD
PHYSICAL MAP

150°   180°   150°   120°   90°   60°

Beaufort
Sea
Banks Is.
Melville Is.
Ellesmere Is.
Victoria Is.
Devon Is.
60°
Arctic Circle
Baffin
Bay
Baffin Is.
GF
150°
Mt. McKinley
6194
Gt. Bear
Lake
Bering
Sea
Alaska
Peninsula
Gulf
of
Alaska
Gt. Slave
Lake
Hudson
Canadian
Aleutian Islands
Queen
Charlotte Is.
Bay
Labrador
Peninsula
Labrador
Sea
Vancouver Is.
L. Winnipeg
Shield
Newfoundland
NORTH
L. Superior
L. Huron
L.Michigan
NORTH
COAST RANGE
180th Meridian
L. Erie
APPALACHIAN MOUNTAINS
ROCKY MOUNTAINS
30°
PACIFIC
Mississippi
ATLANT
Rio Grande
Bermuda
Guadalupe Is.
Florida
Peninsula
OCEAN
SA. MADRE OCCIDENTAL
SA. MADRE ORIENTAL
Tropic of Cancer
Gulf
of Mexico
Cuba
Hispaniola
OCEAN
California Pen.
Greater Antilles
Caribbean Sea
Lesser Antilles
Equator
0°
Galapagos Is.
Isthmus of Panama
Llanos
Orinoco
ANDES
Amazon
Amazon Basin
Fe
Brazilian
Highlands
Is. Sala y Gómez
Desventuradas Is.
Gran Chaco
Paraná
30°
Easter Is.
Mt. Aconcagua
6959
Juan
Fernández
ANDES
Pampas
Argentine Sea
SOUTH
Falkland Is.
PACIFIC
Tierra del Fuego
Cape Horn
OCEAN
Drake Passage
Antarctic Peninsula
150°   60°

KEY

Altitude (in metres)
4000 or over
2000
500
200
0
-200 (depression)

Depth (in metres)
0
-200
-2000
-5000 or over

Scale
0   3000 km

Antarctic Circle
Alexander Is.
Vinson
Massif
4892
Ellsworth Land
Marie Byrd Land
150°   180°   150°   120°   90°   60°

ARCTIC OCEAN

Svalbard

Jan Mayen Is.

North Cape

Novaya
Zemlya

Barents
Sea

Kola
Peninsula

Is.

Norwegian Sea

SCANDINAVIAN MOUNTAINS

North
Sea

British Isles

Baltic Sea

North European Plain

L. Onega

East
European
Plain

URAL MOUNTAINS

Central
Russian
Upland

Volga

New Siberian
Is.

North Siberian Lowland

Arctic Circle

Lena

Central
Siberian
Plateau

KOLYMA MOUNTAINS

Bering
Sea

Kamchatka
Peninsula

Aleutian Islands

ALPS

Mt. Blanc
4810

APENNINES

BALKANS

Danube

Black Sea

Caspian
Sea

Aral
Sea

CAUCASUS

Mt. Elbrus
5642

TIEN SHAN

L. Baikal

YABLONOVY
MOUNTAINS

Amur

Sea
of
Okhotsk

Sakhalin

West
Siberian
Plain

Plateau of
Mongolia

Hokkaido

NORTH

Iberian
Peninsula

Mediterranean Sea

Crete

Anatolian
Plateau

Syrian
Desert

Iranian
Plateau

ALTAI
MOUNTAINS

TIBETAN
PLATEAU

HIMALAYAS

Huang He

Yangtze

Sea
of
Japan

Honshu

Mt. Fuji
3776

Kyushu

East
China
Sea

PACIFIC

ATLAS
MOUNTAINS

Persian Gulf

Indus

Mt. Everest
8848

Tropic of Cancer

OCEAN

30°

SAHARA

Niger

L. Chad

Red Sea

Nile

Libyan Desert

Arabian
Peninsula

Socotra

Arabian
Sea

Ganges

Western Ghats

Deccan
Plateau

Eastern Ghats

Lakshadweep
Is.

Bay of
Bengal

Andaman Is.

Nicobar Is.

Indochinese
Peninsula

Hainan

South
China
Sea

Luzon

Philippine
Sea

Mindanao

Gulf
of
Guinea

Congo

Congo
Basin

L. Tanganyika

Ethiopian
Highlands

Somali
Peninsula

L. Victoria

Mt. Kilimanjaro
5895

L. Malawi

Maldive
Is.

Sri
Lanka

Sumatra

Borneo

Sulawesi

Flores

Java

Timor

Puncak
Jaya
5030

New
Guinea

Coral Sea

Equator

0°

Namib Desert

Kalahari
Desert

Mozambique Channel

Madagascar

INDIAN

OCEAN

Great Sandy
Desert

Simpson
Desert

Great
Victoria
Desert

Darling

Great Barrier Reef

The Great Divide

Tropic of Capricorn

SOUTH

Cape Agulhas

Mt. Kosciusko
2228

30°

TLANTIC

Tasmania

North Island

New
Zealand

South Island

SOUTH

OCEAN

PACIFIC

Greenwich Meridian

OCEAN

Wilkes Land

Antarctic Circle

60°

Queen Maud Land

0° 30° 60° 90° 120° 150° 180° 150°

THE WORLD
POLITICAL MAP

RUSSIA

Arctic Circle

60°

ALASKA
(USA)

Kodiak Is.

Aleutian Islands (USA)

Alexander Arch.

Banks Is.

Melville Is.

Ellesmere Is.

GRE
(De

Devon Is.

Victoria Is.

Baffin Is.

C A N A D A

NORTH

30°

PACIFIC

180th Meridian

60°

UNITED STATES
OF AMERICA

Newfoundland

Ottawa

Washington DC

N O R T

OCEAN

Guadalupe Is.
(Mexico)

HAWAII (USA)

Tropic of Cancer

Honolulu

MEXICO

Mexico City

Havana

CUBA

BAHAMAS

Nassau

DOMINICAN REPUBLIC
Santo Domingo

PUERTO RICO
San Juan

Bermuda
(UK)

ATLAN

OCEA

Belmopan
BELIZE
GUATEMALA
Guatemala City
San Salvador
EL SALVADOR

HONDURAS
Tegucigalpa
NICARAGUA
Managua

JAMAICA
Kingston

HAITI
Port-au-Prince

ST KITTS AND NEVIS
ANTIGUA AND BARBUDA
DOMINICA
ST LUCIA
BARBADOS
GRENADA
TRINIDAD AND TOBAGO
Port of Spain

ST VINCENT

0°

Equator

KIRIBATI

COSTA RICA
San José

PANAMA
Panama City

Caracas
VENEZUELA

Georgetown
GUYANA

Paramaribo
SURINAME

Cayenne
FRENCH
GUIANA

Bogotá
COLOMBIA

Quito

ECUADOR

Galapagos Is.
(Ecuador)

PERU
Lima

B R A Z I L

SAMOA
Apia

AMERICAN SAMOA
Pago Pago

FIJI
Suva

TONGA
Nuku'alofa

Tropic of Capricorn

La Paz
BOLIVIA
Sucre

Brasília

PARAGUAY
Asunción

Is. Sala y Gómez
(Chile)

Easter Is.
(Chile)

30°

CHILE

Juan Fernández
(Chile)

*Santiago
de Chile*

URUGUAY
Montevideo

Buenos Aires

ARGENTINA

NEW
ZEALAND

Wellington

S O U T H

PACIFIC

OCEAN

Falkland Is.
(UK)

South
Georgia
(UK)

S
Sand

Drake Passage

Antarctic Circle

60°

Scale

0   3000 km

A

150°   180°   150°   120°   90°   60°

ARCTIC OCEAN

Svalbard
(Norway)

Novaya
Zemlya

Jan Mayen Is.
(Norway)

RUSSIA

New Siberian Is.

Arctic Circle

ALASKA
(USA)

Aleutian Islands (USA)

180th Meridian

NORWAY
SWEDEN
FINLAND

Helsinki

Oslo
Stockholm

Tallinn
ESTONIA
Riga
LATVIA
LITHUANIA

Moscow

Astana

KAZAKHSTAN

Ulan Bator

MONGOLIA

Hokkaido

NORTH
KOREA

Pyongyang
Beijing

Honshu

JAPAN

Tokyo

NORTH

PACIFIC

OCEAN

30°

UNITED
KINGDOM

Dublin
London
Brussels
Paris
Bern

Copenhagen
DENMARK

NETHERLANDS
BELGIUM
GERMANY
LUXEMBOURG
SWITZERLAND
FRANCE
MONACO

Berlin

Vilnius

Minsk

BELARUS

Warsaw

POLAND

CZECH REP.
Bratislava
AUSTRIA
HUNGARY
Budapest

Kiev

UKRAINE

Chisinau
MOLDOVA
ROMANIA
Bucharest

Bishkek
Tashkent

KYRGYZSTAN

TURKMENISTAN
Ashgabat

UZBEKISTAN

CHINA

SOUTH
KOREA
Seoul

Taipei

TAIWAN

Ryukyu Is.

Tropic of Cancer

PACIFIC

OCEAN

30°

PORTUGAL
SPAIN

Lisbon
Madrid

Corsica
(France)
Sardinia
(Italy)

Balearic Is.
(Spain)

Rome
ITALY
Tirane
GREECE
Athens

Belgrade
Sofia
BULGARIA

TURKEY

Nicosia
CYPRUS
LEBANON
ISRAEL
Jerusalem
Amman
JORDAN

Tbilisi
GEORGIA
ARMENIA
Yerevan
AZERBAIJAN
Baku

Tehran

IRAN

Ankara

Beirut
Damascus
SYRIA
Baghdad
IRAQ

Kabul
AFGHANISTAN
Islamabad

New Delhi

NEPAL
Kathmandu

Thimphu
BHUTAN

BANGLADESH
Dhaka

Hanoi

Luzon
Manila

PHILIPPINES

Mindanao

PALAU
Koror

MOROCCO
Rabat

ALGERIA

TUNISIA
Tunis
Tripoli
LIBYA

Valletta
MALTA
Crete

EGYPT

Cairo

Riyadh
SAUDI
ARABIA

Doha
QATAR
UNITED
ARAB
EMIRATES
Abu Dhabi
Muscat
OMAN

INDIA

MYANMAR
(BURMA)

Yangon

LAOS
Vientiane

THAILAND
Bangkok

Phnom Penh
CAMBODIA

VIETNAM

SRI LANKA
Kotte

MALAYSIA
KUALA LUMPUR
SINGAPORE

BRUNEI
Bander Seri Begawan

Andaman
Is.
(India)
Nicobar
Is.
(India)

Lakshadweep Is.
(India)

MALDIVES
Male

Socotra
(Yemen)

Borneo
Jakarta

Sulawesi

NAURU

Equator

0°

MALI
NIGER
MAURITANIA
Nouakchott
Bamako
BURKINA
FASO
Ouagadougou
COTE
D'IVOIRE
GHANA
Accra
Lome
Porto Novo

CHAD
N'Djamena

SUDAN
Khartoum

ERITREA
Asmara

YEMEN

DJIBOUTI
Djibouti

SOUTH
SUDAN

Addis Ababa
ETHIOPIA

SOMALIA
Mogadishu

SEYCHELLES
Victoria

INDONESIA

PAPUA
NEW GUINEA
Port Moresby

SOLOMON
ISLANDS
Honiara

TUVALU

NIGERIA
Abuja

CENTRAL
AFRICAN REP.
Bangui

CAMEROON
Yaounde

EQUATORIAL GUINEA
Malabo
SAO TOME
& PRINCIPE
GABON
Libreville

DEMOCRATIC
REPUBLIC
OF THE
CONGO
Kinshasa

Brazzaville
CONGO

UGANDA
Kampala
RWANDA
Kigali
BURUNDI
Bujumbura

KENYA
Nairobi

TANZANIA
Dodoma

COMOROS
Moroni

VANUATU
Port Vila

FIJI
Suva

NEW
CALEDONIA
Noumea

ANGOLA
Luanda

ZAMBIA
Lusaka

Lilongwe

MADAGASCAR
Antananarivo

Port Louis
MAURITIUS
Reunion
(France)

INDIAN

OCEAN

AUSTRALIA

Tropic of Capricorn

30°

NAMIBIA
Windhoek

ZIMBABWE
Harare
BOTSWANA
Gaborone
Pretoria
Maputo

MOZAMBIQUE

Mbabane
SWAZILAND
Maseru
LESOTHO

SOUTH
AFRICA

Cape Town

Canberra

NEW
ZEALAND

Wellington

SOUTH

ATLANTIC

OCEAN

SOUTH

PACIFIC

OCEAN

	COUNTRY	CAPITAL
1	MACEDONIA	Skopje
2	MONTENEGRO	Podgorica
3	BOSNIA HERZEGOVINA	Sarajevo
4	CROATIA	Zagreb
5	SLOVENIA	Ljubljana
6	SAN MARINO	San Marino
7	LIECHTENSTEIN	Vaduz
8	LUXEMBOURG	Luxembourg
9	ANDORRA	Andorra la Vella
10	KOSOVO	Pristina
11	BAHRAIN	Manama

Greenwich Meridian

ANTARCTICA

Antarctic Circle

60°

THE EARTH'S MOVEMENTS

Like all the planets in the Solar System, the Earth spins on its own axis and it also orbits the Sun. These two movements cause the difference between day and night and the changing of the seasons.

23.5°
The angle at which the Earth is tilted.

20/21 JUNE
The longest day in the northern hemisphere happens on the summer solstice.

Yearly orbit

The Earth takes 365 days, 5 hours and 48 minutes to orbit the Sun. As the Earth changes position, the seasons and the length of the day and night change too. The winter solstice is the shortest day of the year, while the summer solstice is the longest day. At the equinoxes, day and night are of equal length all over the planet.

SUN

147.5 MILLION KM

22/23 SEPTEMBER
This is the autumn equinox in the northern hemisphere. Day and night are both 12 hours long.

Axis of rotation

21/22 DECEMBER
This is the winter solstice in the northern hemispher It is the shortest day of the year.

Daily rotation

The Earth turns around its own axis each day. This movement causes day and night. It also makes the planet slightly flattened at the poles, and causes ocean currents.

20/21 MARCH
This is the spring
equinox in the
northern hemisphere.
Day and night are the
same length.

Hemispheres

The Earth is divided into two
halves, or hemispheres:
the northern hemisphere and
the southern hemisphere. The
equator is the imaginary line
that separates them. When it
is summer in the north, it is
winter in the south.

152.5 MILLION KM

LEAP YEAR
Every fourth year, the
month of February
has 29 days instead
of 28. This is called a
leap year.

Northern
hemisphere

Equator

Southern
hemisphere

GREENWICH
MERIDIAN

**24:00
HOURS**

West

East

Jet lag
Long-distance flights can cause
jet lag. This is because a change
in time zones can upset our
body's natural rhythm.

3:00

21:00

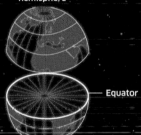

6:00

18:00

↘ Time zones

The Earth is divided into 24 different
time zones by imaginary lines that go
from pole to pole. Each zone's time is one
hour different from its neighbours, with the
Greenwich Meridian at the centre.

9:00

15:00

**12:00
HOURS**

STRUCTURE OF THE EARTH

The Earth is very different under its surface. The rocky ground on which we live is only a thin crust. Underneath the crust is the mantle, made of solid and liquid rock, and in the centre is a hot metal core. The whole planet is surrounded by a layer of gases that form the atmosphere.

How far have we explored?

It is more than 6000 kilometres from the surface to the centre of the Earth. So far, we have managed to explore 12 kilometres down.

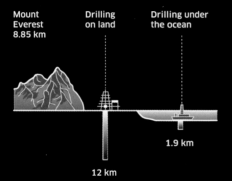

Mount Everest 8.85 km

Drilling on land

Drilling under the ocean

1.9 km

12 km

Outer mantle
The movement of the outer mantle causes earthquakes and volcanoes.

700 KM

2900

2270 KM

1216 KM

Inner core
The inner core is made of solid iron and nickel.

(NOT TO SCALE)

ATMOSPHERE
100 KM

THE EARTH
6370 KM

Outer core
The outer core is made of molten iron and nickel.

Inner mantle
Heavy rocks make up the mantle. They have a temperature of more than 1000 °C.

HOT PLANET
The temperature
of the Earth rises
the closer you get
to the centre.

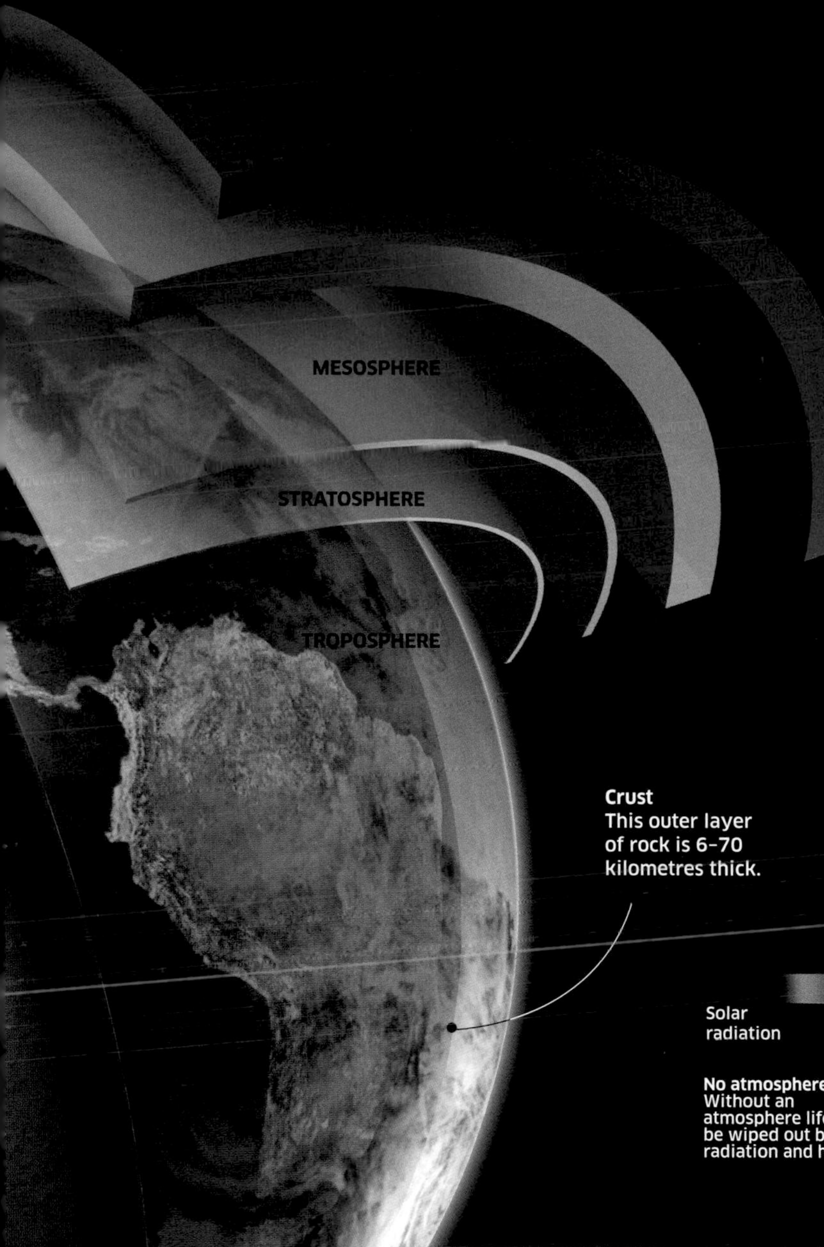

MESOSPHERE

STRATOSPHERE

TROPOSPHERE

Crust
This outer layer
of rock is 6–70
kilometres thick.

The atmosphere

**The atmosphere is made
up of a mixture of gases,
mainly nitrogen and
oxygen. It is divided
into different layers
depending on the amount
of gases at each height.
The atmosphere gives us
the air we breathe and
it protects us from the
Sun's harmful rays.**

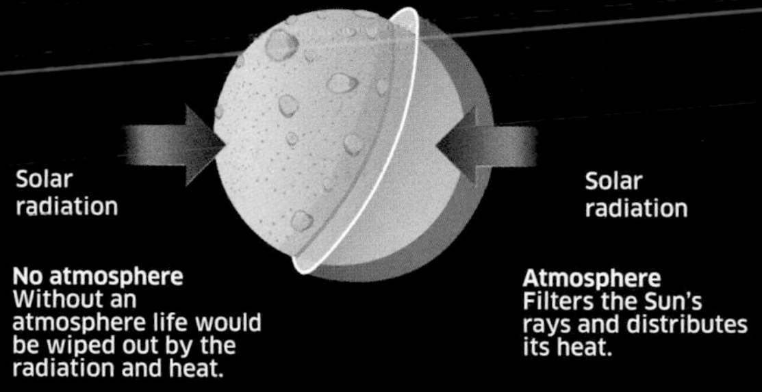

Solar
radiation

Solar
radiation

No atmosphere
Without an
atmosphere life would
be wiped out by the
radiation and heat.

Atmosphere
Filters the Sun's
rays and distributes
its heat.

↘ The hydrosphere

**The hydrosphere is the name for the
liquid part of the Earth, including the
oceans, lakes, rivers, groundwater**

**and water in the atmosphere. Water
covers more than two-thirds of the
Earth's surface.**

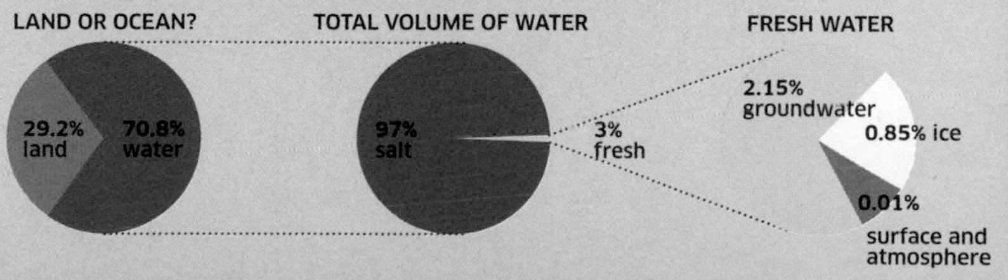

LAND OR OCEAN?

TOTAL VOLUME OF WATER

FRESH WATER

29.2%
land

70.8%
water

97%
salt

3%
fresh

2.15%
groundwater

0.85% ice

0.01%
surface and
atmosphere

THE EARTH'S CRUST

The continents and oceans are found on the Earth's crust. This crust is made up of huge pieces that fit together like a jigsaw puzzle. They are called tectonic plates. These plates float on molten rock, or magma.

NEW ROCKS
When magma from a volcano cools, it forms new rocks in the Earth's crust.

Shaping the Earth's crust

1 Folds
When two plates push together, they form folds. These folds are seen on the surface of the crust as mountains. The Alps, Andes and Rockies are examples of fold mountains.

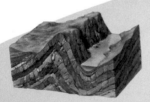

2 Ridges
When two tectonic plates move apart, they leave a gap. This gap is filled with magma from inside the Earth. The magma hardens to form a ridge.

Continental drift
The tectonic plates are continually moving and can move as much as 10 centimetres each year. This movement is called continental drift.

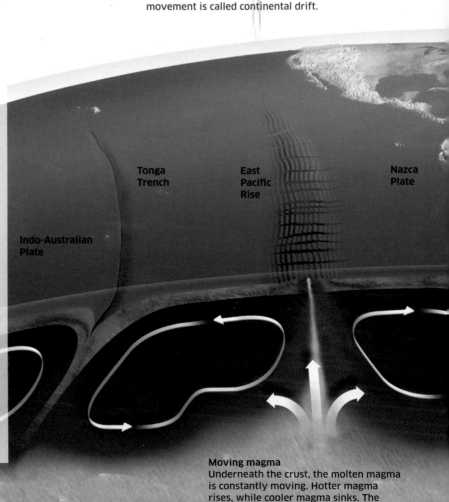

Tonga Trench

East Pacific Rise

Nazca Plate

Indo-Australian Plate

Moving magma
Underneath the crust, the molten magma is constantly moving. Hotter magma rises, while cooler magma sinks. The moving magma drags along the tectonic plates, causing them to move.

70 km

The maximum thickness
of the Earth's crust.

Fault lines

The plates in the
Earth's crust are
separated along
cracks called fault
lines. The rock along
a fault can move
suddenly. When
this happens, we
feel the movement
as an earthquake.

Tectonic plates

**The Earth's crust is made up of
seven major tectonic plates plus
several smaller ones.**

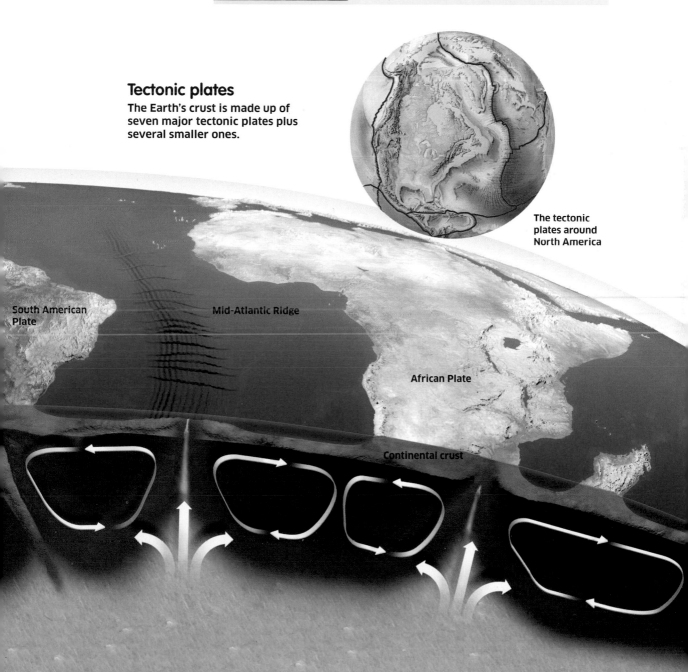

The tectonic
plates around
North America

South American
Plate

Mid-Atlantic Ridge

African Plate

Continental crust

THE OCEANS AND SEAS

Much of the Earth is covered by a large body of salt water, which surrounds the continents. The water forms large, deep oceans and smaller, shallow seas. Underneath the waves, there are huge underwater mountain ranges called ridges, and deep valleys called trenches.

Trenches

The long, steep-sided valleys on the ocean floor are called trenches.

Arctic

Atlantic

Pacific

Indian

Southern

Five oceans

Geographers divide the planet's water into five oceans: Pacific, Atlantic, Indian, Arctic and Southern.

Aleutian Trench
About 3300 km long and more than 7600 m deep, the Aleutian Trench is the world's largest.

Liquid planet

Nearly 71 per cent of the planet's surface is covered with water.

Pacific Ocean
Area: 180 million sq km
Average depth: 4270 m

Atlanic Ocean
Area: 106.4 million sq km
Average depth: 2743 m

Indian Ocean
Area: 75 million sq km
Average depth: 3890 m

Arctic Ocean
Area: 20.3 million sq km
Average depth: 1038 m

Southern Ocean
Area: 14 million sq km
Average depth: 1205 m

Pacific Ocean

The deepest descent

The Bathyscaphe Trieste holds the record for the deepest descent. In 1960, it went down to the Mariana Trench, 10,911 metres below sea level.

East Pacific Rise
The Galapagos Islands and Easter Island lie along this long ocean ridge.

Mid-Atlantic Ridge
This ridge crosses the Atlantic Ocean from north to south. Some of its mountains have emerged as volcanic islands, including the Azores and Iceland.

Ocean life

Most of the planet's life is found in the oceans
and seas. The waters are home to life forms
ranging from the microscopic plankton to the
largest animals of all, whales.

CURRENTS
The ocean currents
are large masses of
cold or hot water
moving through
the oceans.

Blue whale
The largest animal on the
planet, the blue whale
(above), weighs between
100 and 120 tonnes.

Mariana Trench
Located in the Western Pacific,
the Mariana Trench reaches
10,994 m in depth. It is the
deepest trench in the world.

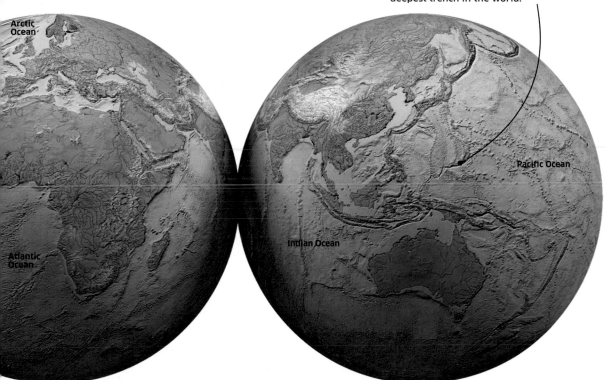

Arctic Ocean

Pacific Ocean

Indian Ocean

Atlantic Ocean

Types of seas

Inland
These seas are
surrounded by
land, such as the
Caspian Sea.

Coastal
Coastal seas are
found in shallow
areas along
continents' coast.

Continental
These seas are
between land,
but have a channel
to the ocean.

THE ARCTIC

The Arctic is the region north of the Arctic Circle. This region includes the northern parts of Asia, North America and Europe, together with most of the world's largest island, Greenland. These land areas enclose the world's smallest ocean, the Arctic Ocean. Near its ice-covered centre is the North Pole.

Icebergs
Icebergs break away from valley glaciers and from Greenland's huge ice sheet. Some drift south into the Atlantic Ocean.

The Inuit

The Inuit live in the Arctic region of North America. In 1999, a new Canadian province named Nunavut was established for them.

A permanently cold region

The Arctic is a bitterly cold region and the Arctic Ocean is largely covered with thick ice throughout the year. Temperatures on the central ice cap can drop below -50 °C, but ocean currents keep the southwestern coast relatively mild.

Greenland

With the exception of Antarctica, Greenland is the world's least-populated land. As well as the Inuit of Greenland and northern Canada, other Arctic peoples are the Sami found in northern Scandinavia, and the Samoyeds, Tungus and Yakuts of northern Asia.

5450 m
The depth of the Arctic Ocean at its deepest.

EXPEDITION
The first expedition to claim to have reached the North Pole was led by Commander Robert Peary in 1909, but many experts now doubt that he actually got there.

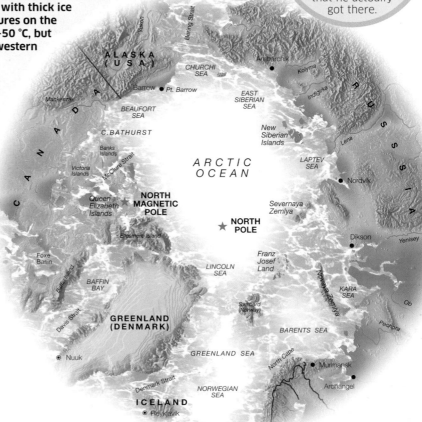

ALASKA (USA)

CANADA

CHURCHI SEA

Ambarchik

Kolyma

Barrow • Pt. Barrow

EAST SIBERIAN SEA

Indigirka

Yukon

Bering Strait

Mackenzie

BEAUFORT SEA

New Siberian Islands

Lena

C. BATHURST

R U S S I A

Banks Islands

McClure Strait

ARCTIC OCEAN

LAPTEV SEA

Victoria Islands

Nordvik

Queen Elizabeth Islands

NORTH MAGNETIC POLE

Severnaya Zemlya

NORTH POLE

Dikson

Yenisey

Ellesmere Island

Foxe Basin

LINCOLN SEA

Franz Josef Land

KARA SEA

Ob

Baffin Island

BAFFIN BAY

Svalbard (Norway)

Novaya Zemlya

Pechora

Davis Strait

GREENLAND (DENMARK)

BARENTS SEA

• Nuuk

GREENLAND SEA

North Cape

• Murmansk

Denmark Strait

NORWEGIAN SEA

Archangel

ICELAND
• Reykjavik

ANIMALS OF THE ARCTIC

HARP SEAL PUPS

Prey of hunters

When they are young, harp seals have soft, white fur. The numbers of seals have dropped because the pups are hunted for this fur.

NORTH AMERICAN CARIBOU

Grazing in the tundra

Caribou are North American deer. They spend the summer grazing on mosses, grasses and lichens in the Arctic tundra.

Tundra

The mainland areas in the Arctic Circle are covered with a treeless wilderness called the tundra. The most common animals are caribou and reindeer, but bears, foxes, hares, lemmings and voles are also found here.

Drying white fish

Although many Arctic people live in settlements today, traditionally they caught different types of fish and hunted seals for food. Fish that was not eaten immediately was hung up to dry and be eaten later.

Icebound ships

The Arctic ice makes shipping conditions difficult. Over the years, ships, including cruise liners and expeditions, have all become stuck in the thick ice.

Animal adaptation

There are several animals found in the Arctic region, including walruses, polar bears, Arctic foxes and birds, such as snowy owls. Plants and animals that live in the Arctic have adapted to help them survive and raise young in the extreme cold and windy conditions. For example, some plants found in the tundra have furry or wax-like coatings to protect them against the cold and wind.

Walrus

A thick layer of special fat, called blubber, keeps walruses warm.

Polar bear

Paw pads with rough surfaces stop polar bears from slipping on the ice.

Arctic fox

An extremely thick, long fur coat keeps the Arctic fox warm.

Snowy owl

The snowy owl has feathers on its legs and feet to provide warmth.

CLIMATE

The Earth's climate is a constantly changing system. It is driven by the energy of the Sun. There are five subsystems to our climate: the atmosphere, the biosphere, the hydrosphere, the cryosphere and the lithosphere. The interactions between these subsystems create different climate zones where the temperature, wind and rain are all similar.

Rain
Water vapour in the atmosphere condenses to form clouds. When the clouds become heavy enough, the water falls as rain or snow.

Atmosphere

Different types of weather are produced here, including rain, wind, water evaporation and humidity.

Biosphere

All living organisms – animals and plants – and their habitats are found here. They give energy to the atmosphere.

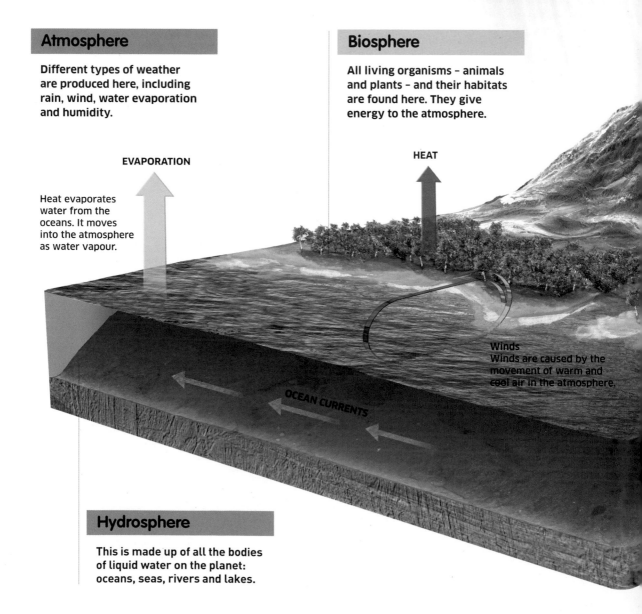

EVAPORATION

HEAT

Heat evaporates water from the oceans. It moves into the atmosphere as water vapour.

Winds
Winds are caused by the movement of warm and cool air in the atmosphere.

OCEAN CURRENTS

Hydrosphere

This is made up of all the bodies of liquid water on the planet: oceans, seas, rivers and lakes.

15 °C
The average temperature at the Earth's surface.

SOLAR RAYS

The Sun
The Sun provides energy and drives the changes in each subsystem.

Lithosphere

The lithosphere is the outer layer of the Earth, formed of the continents and the ocean floor. Continuous changes to its surface affect the climate.

Cryosphere

The cryosphere is the parts of the planet that are covered in ice or where the rock or soil is below 0 °C. It reflects almost all of the Sun's rays back into the atmosphere.

HEAT

HUMAN ACTIVITY

VOLCANOES
The particles that volcanoes put into the atmosphere block out sunlight and lower temperatures.

Return to the sea
Water seeps into the lithosphere and drains through it into the oceans, or the hydrosphere.

Under the volcano
Here, there is molten rock at temperatures of more than 1100 °C.

FLORA AND FAUNA

The Earth is divided into different biomes. A biome is an area with a particular climate in which the plants and animals that live there are adapted to the conditions. Different biomes include grassland, tundra and desert. Factors such as the quality of the soil, altitude and human activity can affect how each species lives within each biome.

Polar bears
When ice forms over the ocean, polar bears move onto the ice to hunt.

Climate

The Earth's biomes are divided according to the climate in which they are found. Climatic conditions such as wind, temperature and rainfall determine which organisms live in each biome. Some plants and animals have developed specifically to survive in a certain biome. However, some animals are forced to migrate to different biomes with better living conditions.

Distribution
Plants and animals need water to survive. Fewer species are found in habitats where there is less water. These are the world's deserts.

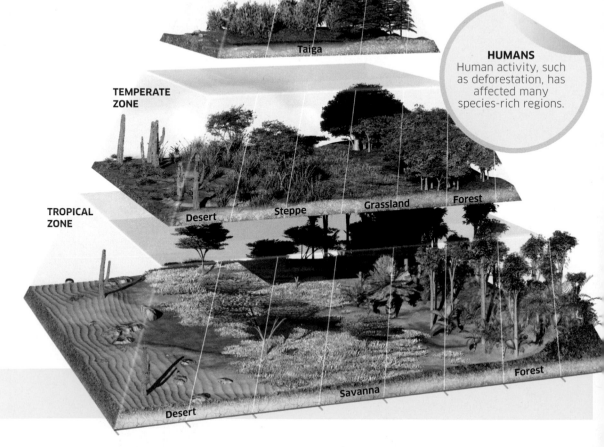

POLAR ZONE

Tundra

SUBPOLAR ZONE

Taiga

HUMANS
Human activity, such as deforestation, has affected many species-rich regions.

TEMPERATE ZONE

Desert   Steppe   Grassland   Forest

TROPICAL ZONE

Desert   Savanna   Forest

Animal adaptation

Animals have adapted to live in certain biomes. These adaptations ensure their survival. However, when human activity causes changes to their natural habitats, animals find that they have smaller and smaller regions in which to live.

Deserts

Many of the animals that live in deserts, such as the spiny lizard (above), can survive for days on very little food or water.

Polar regions

Very few species are found in the icy polar regions. Polar bears (above) have a special thick coat to protect them from the cold.

Marine biodiversity

There is a wide variety of species in the world's oceans and seas. Large numbers of species are found in the world's warm tropical waters.

Tropical forests

The tropical forests are home to many different species. This tree frog feeds on crickets, flies and moths.

Biomes of the world

This map shows the different biomes found on land and in the water.

- Mountains
- Desert
- Grassland
- Taiga
- Temperate forests
- Tropical rainforests
- Polar
- Coral reefs

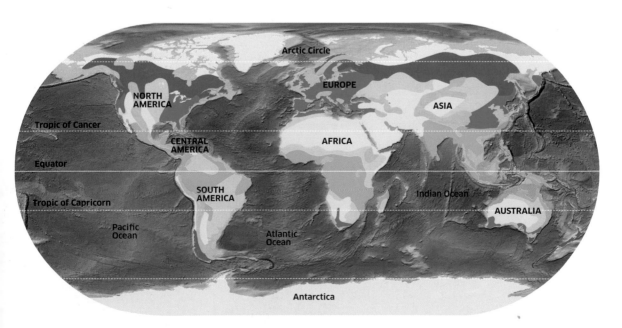

ANTARCTICA

The Antarctic lies south of the Antarctic Circle. It includes most of the world's fifth-largest continent, Antarctica, in the middle of which is the South Pole. Only the tip of the Antarctic Peninsula, jutting out towards South America, lies outside the Antarctic Circle. The waters around Antarctica are called the Southern Ocean or Antarctic Ocean.

INTERNATIONAL PARK?
Many people would like to make Antarctica a protected area, keeping it safe from development.

Antarctic Circle

Ice covers about 98 per cent of Antarctica. The average thickness of the ice is 2200 metres, but in places it is 4800 metres thick. The region is so cold that there are few plants and animals that can survive the icy temperatures. However, the region is home to penguins. These flightless birds feed mainly on the fish they find in the waters around the continent.

S. Orkney Is.
C. Norvegia
Queen Maud Land
S. Shetland Is.
WEDDELL SEA
Coats Land
Enderby Land
Antarctic Peninsula
Palmer Archipelago
Mac Robertson Land
Berkner Is.
CAPE DARNLEY
Alexander Is.
RONNE ICE SHELF
PENSACOLA MTNS.
PR. CHARLES MTNS.
Charcot Is.
AMERICAN HIGHLAND
BELLINGHAUSEN SEA
Vinson Massif 4892
SOUTH POLE
GREATER ANTARCTICA
Queen Mary Land
Ellsworth Land
LESSER ANTARCTICA
TRANSANTARCTIC MTNS.
Knox Coast
Thurston Is.
AMUNDSEN SEA
Mt. Kirkpatric 4528
Siple Is.
Mary Byrd Land
ROSS ICE SHELF
Wilkes Land
Roosevelt Is.
Victoria Land
Mt. Erebus 3794
ROSS SEA
George V Land
C. Adare
SOUTH MAGNETIC POLE

Exploring the Antarctic

Early explorers in Antarctica faced great hardship. An expedition first reached the South Pole in 1911. It was led by the Norwegian Roald Amundsen. A British expedition led by Robert Falcon Scott reached the South Pole five weeks later, but Scott and all his team died on the way back.

-89.2 °C

The coldest temperature ever recorded was at the Russian Vostok Station.

Roald Amundsen
In 1911, Amundsen was the first man to reach the South Pole. In 1926, he took part in an expedition that flew over the North Pole. He disappeared in June 1928 while on a rescue mission.

Whopping whale
Blue whales, the largest living animals, feed on krill found in the seas around Antarctica.

Trawling near Antarctica
The cold waters around Antarctica are rich in marine life, including krill (tiny, shrimp-like creatures), squid, seals, fish and whales. An abundance of fish means the area has excellent trawling conditions.

Tents in the snow
Scientists exploring Antarctica use specially-designed tents called 'Scott's Polar Tents', which are very durable and keep in the heat.

Penguin parade Adélie penguins, the most common penguins in Antarctica, build nests of pebbles on the coast.

Wandering albatross
Found around the Southern Ocean, these birds feed mainly on squid, fish and krill. They have the widest wingspan of any living bird at 3.7 metres.

RESEARCH AND EXPLORATION

Ice cave Around the coast of Antarctica, the sea hollows out spectacular caves in the ice.

OZONE LAYER HOLES

Blocking harmful rays
The ozone layer in the Earth's upper atmosphere blocks most of the Sun's ultraviolet rays. Pollution has created holes in the ozone layer over Antarctica. Research is being done to work out how this affects the region.

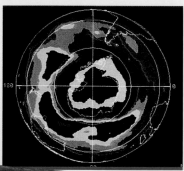

SCIENTISTS IN ANTARCTICA

Vital supplies
There are several research centres in Antarctica. Some have scientists working there all year round, while others are used just in the summer months. Every day, supplies for these scientists are flown or shipped in to Antarctica.

Weather balloons
Balloons sent up into the atmosphere are used to study weather conditions. The balloons sent up in Antarctica are important because conditions there affect the world's weather.

POPULATION

In 2011, the number of people in the world (the world's population) exceeded 7 billion. However, these people are not spread across the planet evenly. Some areas, such as parts of China, India and Europe, are densely populated, while other regions such as Australia and Greenland have far fewer people living in them.

HUNGER
According to the United Nations, 925 million people in the world do not have enough to eat.

THE 20 MOST-POPULOUS COUNTRIES

1. China 1,343,239,923
2. India 1,205,073,612
3. United States of America 313,847,465
4. Indonesia 248,216,193
5. Brazil 205,716,890
6. Pakistan 190,291,129
7. Nigeria 170,123,740
8. Bangladesh 161,083,804
9. Russia 138,082,178
10. Japan 127,368,088
11. Mexico 114,975,406
12. Philippines 103,775,002
13. Ethiopia 93,815,992
14. Vietnam 91,519,289
15. Egypt 83,688,164
16. Germany 81,305,856
17. Turkey 79,749,461
18. Iran 78,868,711
19. Dem. Republic of Congo 73,599,190
20. Thailand 67,091,089

Population Density

A country's population density is the average number of people living on each square kilometre of land.

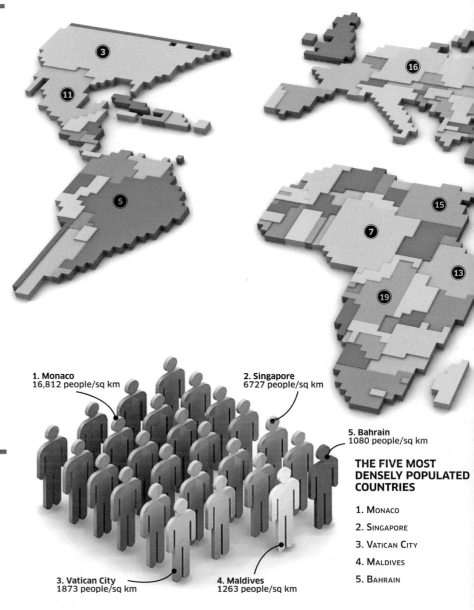

1. Monaco
16,812 people/sq km

2. Singapore
6727 people/sq km

5. Bahrain
1080 people/sq km

3. Vatican City
1873 people/sq km

4. Maldives
1263 people/sq km

THE FIVE MOST DENSELY POPULATED COUNTRIES

1. MONACO
2. SINGAPORE
3. VATICAN CITY
4. MALDIVES
5. BAHRAIN

CASE STUDIES
CITY AND COUNTRY

Migration

Migration is the word used for the movement of people from one place to another, both within the same country or from one country to another. People may move in search of work or to leave a war-torn area.

Urbanization

People often migrate from the countryside to live in cities or towns. This is called urbanization. Trinidad and Tobago in the Caribbean has a very low level of urbanization. Just 13 per cent of people live in cities or towns.

40%

The predicted increase in world population by 2050, according to the United Nations.

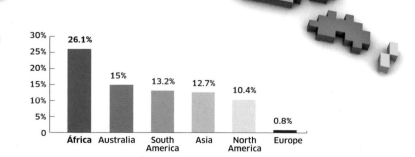

THE THREE MAIN RELIGIONS IN THE WORLD

1. CHRISTIANITY
2.1 BILLION FOLLOWERS

2. ISLAM
1.5 BILLION FOLLOWERS

3. HINDUISM
900 MILLION FOLLOWERS

POPULATION GROWTH 2000–2010

The world's population is growing fastest in less economically developed areas. Many rich parts of the world are already very densely populated.

Region	Growth
África	26.1%
Australia	15%
South America	13.2%
Asia	12.7%
North America	10.4%
Europe	0.8%

THE MODERN WORLD

In recent centuries, human activity has been changing the planet. Large areas of forest have been cut down to make way for farms, while pollution from industry is harming the atmosphere. This is having a serious effect on the environment, and in coming years, we will need to find new ways to live that are less harmful to the planet we depend on.

CARBON
The level of carbon dioxide in the atmosphere has increased by 40 per cent in the last 150 years.

 NEOLITHIC
Humans first started to farm about 10,000 years ago. The farmers built towns to live in and for the first time people settled in one place rather than moving around as nomads.

3 INDUSTRIAL AGE
The Industrial Age saw more people living in cities and more manufacturing. The manufacturing caused an increase in pollution.

Distanced from nature

More people than ever before live in cities, human-made environments that are far from nature. As the population grows, new cities are being built. It is important that cities are planned to make them energy-efficient, meaning that people use less energy to heat their homes and travel to work.

 MIDDLE AGES
During the Middle Ages, the walled cities of Europe were very crowded and people lived in poor conditions.

7 billion

The world's population in 2011. A thousand years ago, there were only 300 million people, the population of the United States today.

400 million

The estimated number of dogs in the world.

22,000

The estimated number of polar bears in the world.

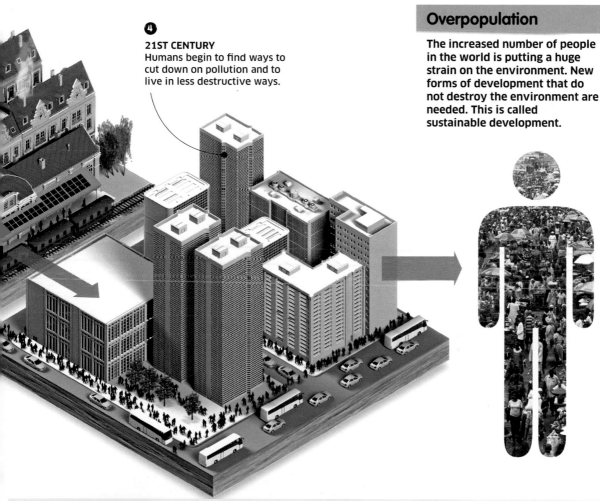

❹

21ST CENTURY
Humans begin to find ways to cut down on pollution and to live in less destructive ways.

Overpopulation

The increased number of people in the world is putting a huge strain on the environment. New forms of development that do not destroy the environment are needed. This is called sustainable development.

Threats

Overpopulation is the root of many problems, including hunger, climate change, pollution and the destruction of wildlife.

CLIMATE CHANGE

In recent years, the average temperature of the Earth has been slowly rising. This increase in average temperature is called global warming. The main cause of global warming is human activity. While the change in temperature both on land and in the sea has been gradual, global warming is changing the world's climate, which is causing serious problems in some parts of the world.

CORAL REEFS
Many coral reefs are dying because of the increase in sea temperature.

THE EFFECTS OF GLOBAL WARMING

The global temperature has increased by a few tenths of a degree in the last few decades. Although this seems like a small change, life on the Earth is delicately balanced, and a small change in temperature can have a serious effect. Global warming has become a major threat to the welfare of all living beings.

50%

The reduction in population of Adélie penguins because of ice loss in Antarctica in the last 30 years.

Thawing at the poles
The rise in temperature is causing large amounts of ice at the polar caps to melt. This leads to an increase in sea level.

Floods
Climate change is causing large floods. In recent years, Bangladesh has seen some of the worst floods in its history.

Islands under the water
The small Pacific islands of Tuvalu and Kiribati and the Maldives in the Indian Ocean are very low-lying, which makes them vulnerable to rising sea levels. If the oceans rise just a couple of metres, this will leave the islands completely underwater.

Disappearing glaciers
As a result of global warming, many glaciers in mountainous regions are shrinking.

Desertification
Climate change is causing drought in central Asia. This leads to poor harvests and a shortage of food.

Greenhouse effect

Greenhouses are specially built to trap heat so that plants can be grown. Similarly, the greenhouse effect is a natural process where the gases in the Earth's atmosphere trap some of the Sun's energy. Without the greenhouse effect, the planet would be too cold to live on.

Carbon dioxide and methane are both greenhouse gases. Carbon dioxide is given off when coal, gas and oil are burned. Methane is given off by cattle. Increases in the level of both of these gases in the atmosphere means that the average temperature of the Earth is increasing.

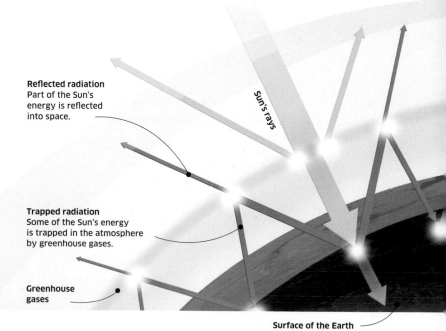

Reflected radiation
Part of the Sun's energy is reflected into space.

Sun's rays

Trapped radiation
Some of the Sun's energy is trapped in the atmosphere by greenhouse gases.

Greenhouse gases

Surface of the Earth

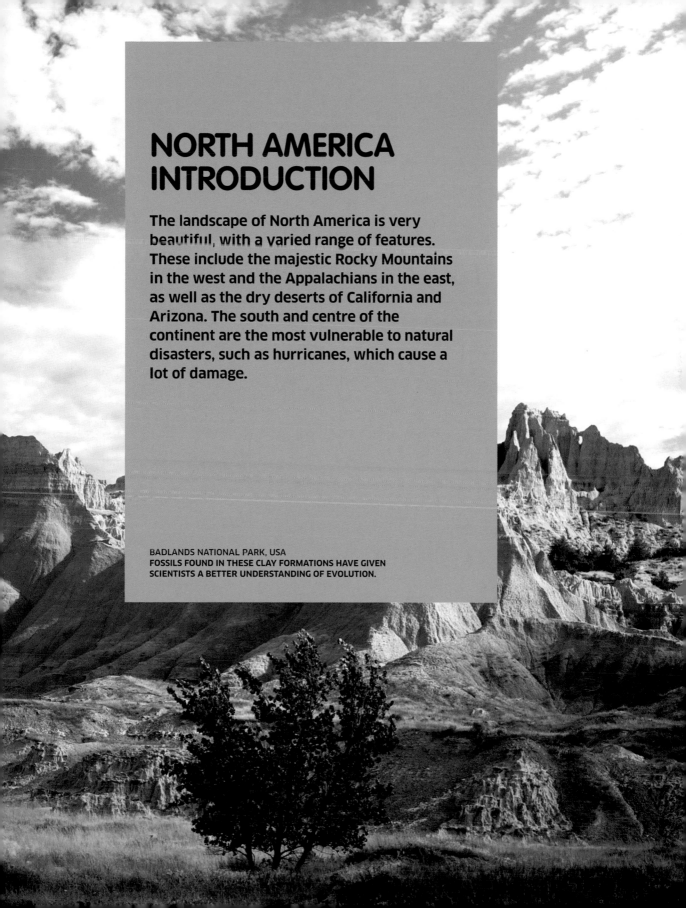

NORTH AMERICA INTRODUCTION

The landscape of North America is very beautiful, with a varied range of features. These include the majestic Rocky Mountains in the west and the Appalachians in the east, as well as the dry deserts of California and Arizona. The south and centre of the continent are the most vulnerable to natural disasters, such as hurricanes, which cause a lot of damage.

BADLANDS NATIONAL PARK, USA
FOSSILS FOUND IN THESE CLAY FORMATIONS HAVE GIVEN
SCIENTISTS A BETTER UNDERSTANDING OF EVOLUTION.

NORTH AMERICA
PHYSICAL MAP

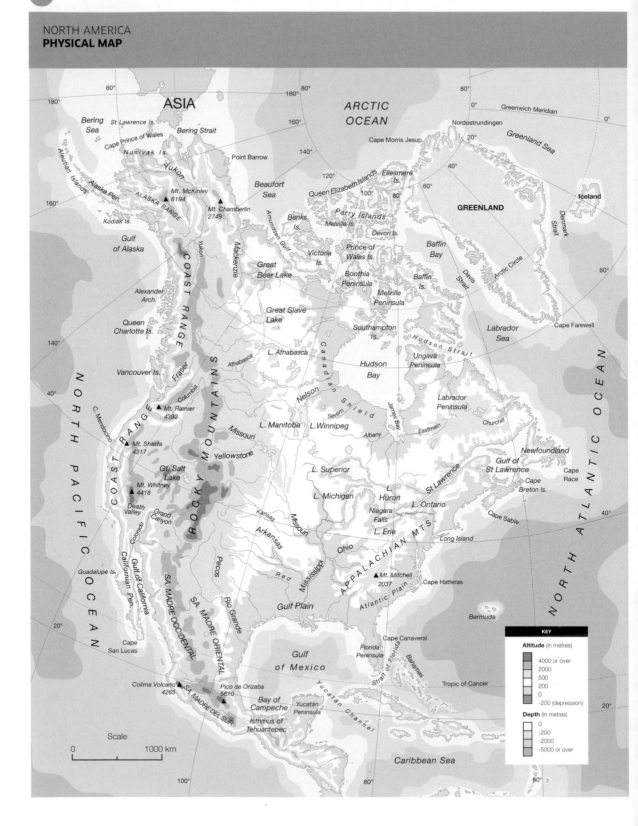

ASIA

ARCTIC OCEAN

Greenwich Meridian

Bering Sea

St Lawrence Is.

Cape Prince of Wales

Bering Strait

Nunivak Is.

Point Barrow

Nordostrundingen

Cape Morris Jesup

Greenland Sea

Aleutian Islands

Alaska Pen.

ALASKA RANGE

Yukon

▲ Mt. McKinley 6194

▲ Mt. Chamberlin 2749

Beaufort Sea

Queen Elizabeth Islands

Ellesmere Is.

GREENLAND

Iceland

Denmark Strait

Kodiak Is.

Gulf of Alaska

Mackenzie

Banks Is.

Melville Is.

Parry Islands

Devon Is.

Prince of Wales Is.

Baffin Bay

Arctic Circle

Alexander Arch.

Great Bear Lake

Victoria Is.

Boothia Peninsula

Melville Peninsula

Baffin Is.

Davis Strait

Cape Farewell

Queen Charlotte Is.

COAST RANGE

Great Slave Lake

Southampton Is.

Hudson Strait

Labrador Sea

Vancouver Is.

Fraser

Yukon

L. Athabasca

Canadian Shield

Hudson Bay

Ungava Peninsula

NORTH

Athabasca

Nelson

Labrador Peninsula

Columbia

C. Mendocino

▲ Mt. Rainier 4392

ROCKY MOUNTAINS

Severn

James Bay

Churchill

▲ Mt. Shasta 4317

Missouri

Yellowstone

L. Manitoba

L. Winnipeg

Albany

Eastmain

Newfoundland

Gt. Salt Lake

L. Superior

St. Lawrence

Gulf of St Lawrence

Cape

Cape Race

PACIFIC

▲ Mt. Whitney 4418

Death Valley

Grand Canyon

Kansas

L. Michigan

L. Huron

L. Ontario

Niagara Falls

Breton Is.

Cape Sable

COAST RANGE

Colorado

Missouri

L. Erie

APPALACHIAN MTS.

Long Island

NORTH ATLANTIC OCEAN

Guadalupe Is.

Gulf of California

Arkansas

Ohio

SA. MADRE OCCIDENTAL

Pecos

Atlantic Plain

OCEAN

Red

Mississippi

▲ Mt. Mitchell 2037

Cape Hatteras

Cape San Lucas

California Pen.

SA. MADRE ORIENTAL

Rio Grande

Gulf Plain

Bermuda

Cape Canaveral

Florida Peninsula

Colima Volcano 4265 ▲

SA. MADRE DEL SUR

Pico de Orizaba 5610 ▲

Bay of Campeche

Gulf of Mexico

Yucatán Peninsula

Bahamas

Strait of Florida

Tropic of Cancer

Yucatán Channel

Isthmus of Tehuantepec

Caribbean Sea

Scale

0   1000 km

KEY

Altitude (in metres)

4000 or over
2000
500
200
0
-200 (depression)

Depth (in metres)

0
-200
-2000
-5000 or over

NORTH AMERICA
POLITICAL MAP

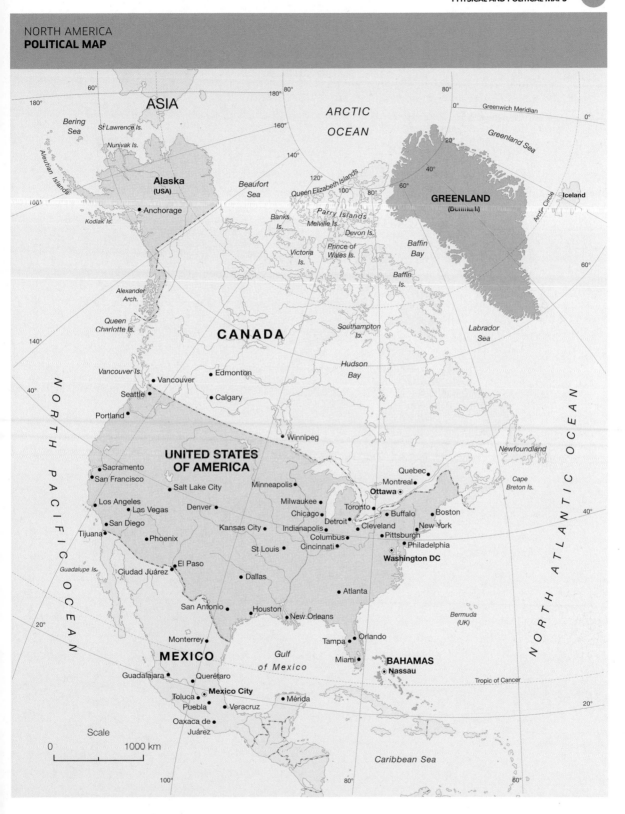

ASIA

ARCTIC OCEAN

Greenwich Meridian

Bering Sea

St Lawrence Is.

Nunivak Is.

Aleutian Islands

Greenland Sea

Alaska (USA)

Beaufort Sea

Queen Elizabeth Islands

Greenland

Anchorage

Kodiak Is.

Banks Is.

Parry Islands

Melville Is.

Devon Is.

GREENLAND
(Denmark)

Iceland

Arctic Circle

Victoria Is.

Prince of Wales Is.

Baffin Bay

Baffin Is.

Alexander Arch.

Queen Charlotte Is.

CANADA

Southampton Is.

Labrador Sea

Vancouver Is.

Hudson Bay

Vancouver

Edmonton

Seattle

Calgary

Portland

Winnipeg

Newfoundland

UNITED STATES OF AMERICA

Quebec

Cape Breton Is.

Sacramento

Montreal

San Francisco

Salt Lake City

Minneapolis

Ottawa

Los Angeles

Milwaukee

Toronto

Buffalo

Boston

Las Vegas

Denver

Chicago

Detroit

Cleveland

New York

San Diego

Kansas City

Indianapolis

Pittsburgh

Tijuana

Columbus

Philadelphia

Phoenix

St Louis

Cincinnati

Washington DC

Guadalupe Is.

El Paso

Ciudad Juárez

Dallas

Atlanta

Bermuda (UK)

San Antonio

Houston

New Orleans

Monterrey

Tampa

Orlando

MEXICO

Gulf of Mexico

Miami

BAHAMAS

Nassau

Guadalajara

Querétaro

Tropic of Cancer

Toluca

Mexico City

Mérida

Puebla

Veracruz

Oaxaca de Juárez

NORTH PACIFIC OCEAN

NORTH ATLANTIC OCEAN

Caribbean Sea

Scale

0   1000 km

THE ROCKY MOUNTAINS

This mountain chain, also known as the Rockies, runs parallel to the west coast of North America, covering over 4800 kilometres. The mountains sweep down from northwest Canada to the southwestern United States. They are a popular tourist destination, especially for hiking, camping, fishing, mountain biking, skiing and snowboarding.

VISITS
More than 3 million visitors go to the Rocky Mountain National Park every year.

Four regions

The Rockies border the Great Plains to the east and the Rocky Mountain Trench to the west. The mountains are sometimes divided into four sections (right). This includes the Brooks Range, which extends from Canada into Alaska, and is often thought of as an extension of the Rockies.

Labrador Seaway

Hudson Seaway

Western Interior Seaway

Where they came from

The Rockies are young mountains that formed 75 million years ago. They first appeared when the ocean floor emerged out of the sea in a great arch.

Arctic Province
The Alaska Range is home to North America's highest peak, Mount McKinley, which sits at 6194 m.

Northern Province
From British Columbia, the Rockies stretch through Canada and continue into the US states of Washington, Idaho and Wyoming. This part of the chain is extremely rugged and beautiful, with glaciers in some areas. Mount Robson (3954 m) is the highest peak in this region.

Central Province
This region includes Wyoming and its highest peak is Gannett Peak at 4207 m.

Southern Province
This area has the highest elevation of the Rockies. Its highest peak is Mount Elbert at 4399 m.

Alaska Range

Brooks Range

Mount McKinley

ALASKA

CANADA

Mount Robson

Gannett Peak

UNITED STATES

Profile

This profile of the Southern Province Rockies gives an impression of the majestic peaks of the mountains.

■ The Rockies

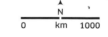

N

0   km   1000

Comanche Peak 3872 m

Electric Peak 3343 m

Mount Raddle 3726 m

Pikes Peak 4300 m

Mount Logan 3923 m

Mount Evans 4348 m

Longs Peak 4345 m

Ypsilon 4117 m

Bald Mountain 3354 m

Bald Chiquita Mountain 2998 m

THE APPALACHIANS

The most prominent feature of the landscape in eastern North America is the Appalachian mountain range. These fold mountains formed around 480 million years ago. Mount Mitchell is the highest peak, at 2037 metres.

MINING

Mining in this mountain area is threatening wildlife.

Colourful highlands
Small, colourful shrubs cover the highlands of Appalachia.

American holly

With its bright red berries, American holly is found in the region.

Cottontail rabbit

The cottontail rabbit is one of the most common inhabitants of the region.

FACT FILE

Mount Mitchell

Located in North Carolina, east of the Mississippi, Mount Mitchell is the highest point of the Appalachians.

Fauna and flora

The mountains are home to many different plant and animal species. The most common animals found in the mountains include black bears, deer and elk, as well as numerous insects and rodents.

Susquehanna River

The Susquehanna River runs through the Appalachians. Its source is in New York State and it crosses through Pennsylvania and Maryland.

MOUNT ST HELENS

One of the most explosive volcanoes in North America, Mount St Helens, is found in Washington State. Mount St Helens was inactive for many years but on 18 May 1980, it erupted. The eruption killed 57 people and there were avalanches of lava that destroyed 600 square kilometres of trees. The nearby lake overflowed causing mudslides that destroyed houses and highways.

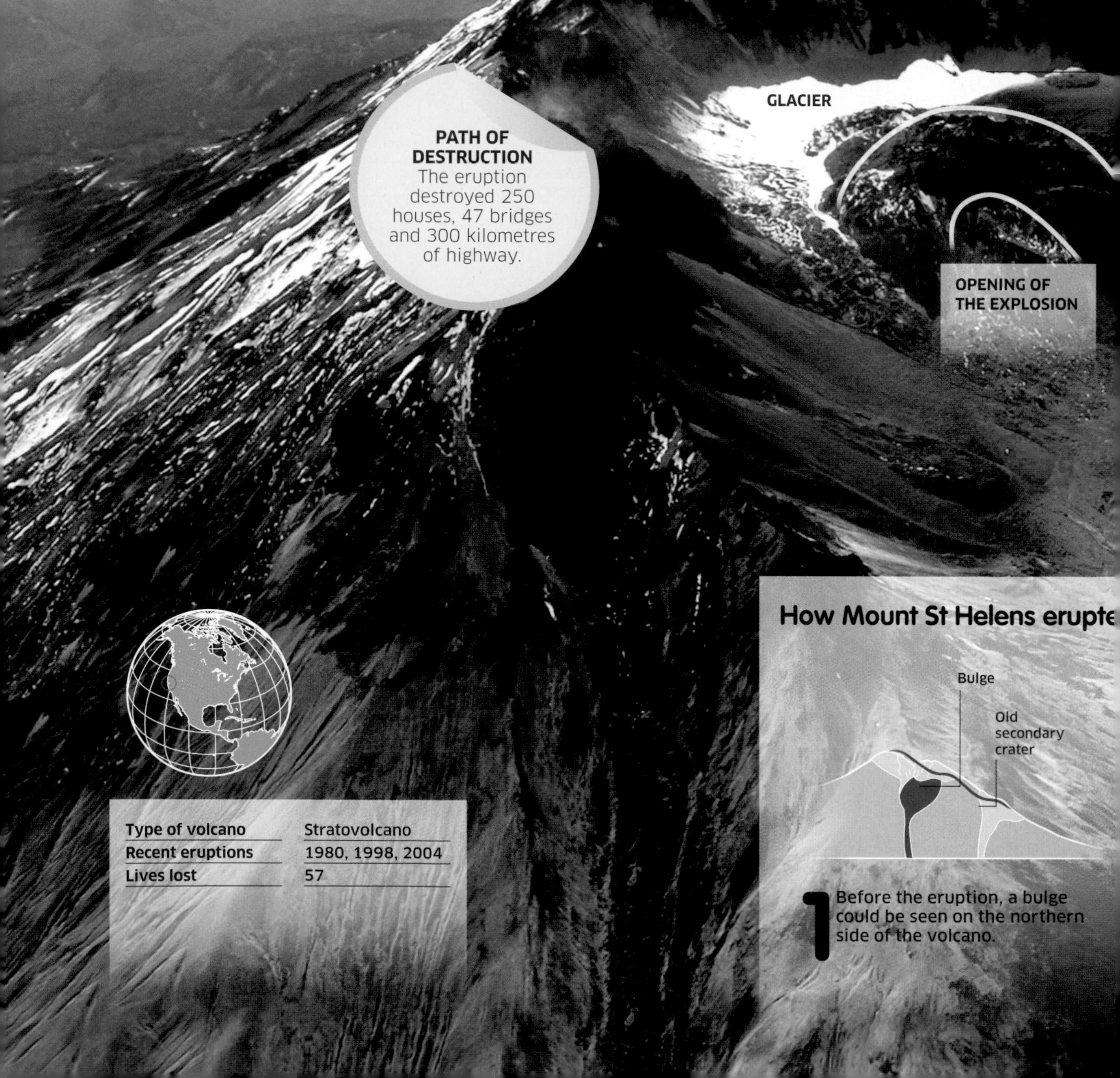

PEAK BEFORE THE EXPLOSION

GLACIER

PATH OF DESTRUCTION
The eruption destroyed 250 houses, 47 bridges and 300 kilometres of highway.

OPENING OF THE EXPLOSION

Type of volcano	Stratovolcano
Recent eruptions	1980, 1998, 2004
Lives lost	57

How Mount St Helens erupte

Bulge

Old secondary crater

1 Before the eruption, a bulge could be seen on the northern side of the volcano.

2950 m

After the eruption,
Mount St Helens
lost its cone shape.

-401 m

2549 m

THE ERUPTION OF MOUNT ST HELENS

Before and after the eruption

Mount St Helens was a striking feature of the landscape. Before the eruption, forests and fields surrounded the volcano. The eruption left the top of the volcano as a horseshoe-shaped pit, with nothing around it.

During the explosion

The energy released was many times more powerful than an atomic bomb. The explosion lasted more than nine hours.

Volcanic ash burned trees and destroyed forests for several kilometres.

Crater is blocked

The magma could not escape and pressure built up on the northern side

The cone became blocked

The crater explodes

The blockages caused an avalanche of magma and ash

A column of smoke and ash rose 19 km in height

Profile before eruption

Profile after eruption

2 Pressure built up on the northern side.

3 Magma and gases erupted in a huge explosion.

4 The ash eruption appeared at its most powerful.

THE SEMI-DESERT HABITAT

Rainfall is rare in the semi-desert, but the small amount of precipitation is what makes the difference between this habitat and a desert. The moisture ensures that cactuses, shrubs and many other plants can grow. The abundance of these plants at certain times of the year, especially in spring and summer, attracts animal species. In winter, it is very cold and dry, and the wildlife hibernates or seeks shelter.

LOCATION
Semi-deserts are found in Colorado, Texas and Montana in the United States.

Storing water

Plants with leaves and thick stems, or roots close to the surface, can absorb moisture easily from the rare rainfalls. The cacti leaves will change to thorns, minimizing the moisture they lose and protecting them from hungry animals.

Red-tailed hawk

Gila woodpecker

Elf owl

Pygmy fox

White-tailed squirrel

Tarantula

Ant

Roadrunner
This creature is able to reach a speed of 30 km/h to capture its prey of birds, rodents and reptiles.

American badger

Western diamondback rattlesnake

Saguaro cactus
This cactus's fleshy stem expands like a musical accordion to store water at a volume of 80 per cent of its weight. Its stem may reach a height of nearly 14 metres and it can weigh up to 10 tonnes. Its roots are shallow but can extend up to 30 metres.

The American semi-desert

In winter, the temperature in a semi-desert habitat can drop to -30 °C. These harsh conditions cause animals living there to use the vegetation and cactuses as places to shelter. They also provide a source of water.

Coyote

Musk hog

Black-tailed jackrabbit

Desert tortoise

Gila monster

Desert scorpion
This creature has a weapon in its tail that injects venom into its prey.

THE SEMI-DESERTS OF NORTH AMERICA

Overview
In the semi-desert habitat, only moisture-storing plants, such as cactuses, can survive on the small amount of available moisture. A little more than 250 millilitres of rain falls each year.

Plants
Desert plants flourish in this habitat. The ocotillo (below) sheds its leaves once it has absorbed enough moisture to survive, leaving thorns to protect it.

Wildlife
An adult desert tortoise can survive without water for almost a year. Its front legs are specially adapted to dig large, deep burrows, from which it comes out to feed in the morning and evening. It can live for between 50 and 80 years.

OIL EXPLOSION

On 20 April 2010, BP's oil rig Deepwater Horizon exploded in the Gulf of Mexico, 70 kilometres off the coast of New Orleans, and sank two days later. Until the well was sealed in September, thousands of litres of oil spilled into the ocean each day, having a devastating effect on the environment.

Oil spill
US officials were quick to establish barriers in order to prevent the spill reaching the coast.

DISPERSANTS OF OIL

How they work
Chemical dispersants are used to help clean up oil spills. They quickly break the oil down into natural substances.

The dispersant, which contains cleaning chemicals, is applied.

The chemicals get into the oil.

The chemicals reduce the surface tension of the oil.

Oil droplets start to emerge from the layer.

A shiny coat is left once the oil has been broken down.

TEAMWORK
CLEANING THE COAST

The battle
The success of cleaning up an oil spill depends largely on good organization and teamwork. Sometimes, the oil can be contained using sandbags (right).

Cleaners
To remove oil from coastal rocks, high-pressure washers can be used (right).

Ecological Disaster
The Deepwater Horizon extracted oil from the seabed.

OIL SPILL
NATURAL DISASTER

Fisheries closed

In Louisiana, oysters and shrimp had to be thrown away because they were exposed to oil (below).

Special volunteers

Volunteers helped to clean the feathers of pelicans found off the coast of Louisiana.

Environmental awareness

Environmentalists around the world protested (below) to express their anger over the Gulf of Mexico spill.

Long-term poison

The oil spill has harmed deep-water species, such as sea turtles (below), which migrate to the Mexican coast.

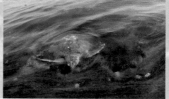

CLIMATE

The North American climate can be extreme and very varied – from the icy temperatures of Alaska, to the dry heat of the deserts of Mexico and the southwestern United States. There are also frequent hurricanes and tornadoes.

Hurricane Katrina Severe floods followed the New Orleans hurricane in 2005.

HURRICANE KATRINA

In the Gulf of Mexico

Starting in the Gulf of Mexico in August 2005, Hurricane Katrina was one of the most powerful tropical storms to hit the USA.

Flooding in New Orleans

The strong winds caused by Katrina flooded New Orleans and submerged much of the city (below).

TORNADOES
TEXAS

Swirling air

Tornadoes are common in the state of Texas. They appear as a column of hot air destroying everything in their path.

THUNDER AND LIGHTNING
GULF OF MEXICO

Moisture and heat

The Gulf of Mexico causes an excess of heat and moisture in its atmosphere. When hot air collides with cold air, thunderstorms form.

WEATHER ALERT
UNITED STATES

Traffic chaos

When there is an extreme weather alert, people are told to leave their homes and to travel to a place of safety. This causes traffic problems.

Anza-Borrego State Park
This park in the Californian desert is home to plants that can tolerate drought.

Coyote

The coyote is a skilful hunter perfectly adapted to the desert environment.

Snakes

Poisonous rattlesnakes are found in the desert areas of the United States.

DESERTS
UNITED STATES

Red Rock Canyon Park
Wind and rain have been eroding the landscape of Red Rock Park for some time (below). The striking formations have been used as the backdrop for many films.

Chihuahuan Desert
One of the largest deserts in North America is the Chihuahaun (below). Its temperatures are extreme with low temperatures in the winter and very hot summers.

Cozumel, Mexico
The island of Cozumel is located 18 kilometres off the coast of Yucatan. Ocean currents in the Gulf of Mexico cause mild temperatures of about 26 °C, making it a popular tourist destination. It is home to several unique animal species, including the dwarf raccoon.

POPULATION AND ECONOMY

According to the Census Bureau of the United States, the total population in 2012 was 313,136,227, and its population growth is among the highest in industrialized countries. Canada and the United States are highly industrialized countries and are considered global powers.

Capitol Hill
This is one of the most iconic buildings in Washington DC.

Capitol

The Capitol Building in Washington DC has housed the meeting chambers of the House of Representatives and the Senate for two centuries.

UNITED STATES
HUMAN GEOGRAPHY

Miami, Florida
Miami (below) is one of the most densely populated cities in the United States, along with New York City.

Cape Canaveral
Cape Canaveral is the main centre for US space activities. It is located on the Atlantic coast of Florida.

Silicon Valley, California
High-tech industries have flourished in Silicon Valley, California. The area includes the Santa Clara Valley and the southern half of the Peninsula of San Francisco.

Palace of Fine Arts
Located in the
historic centre
of Mexico City.

MEXICO
FEDERAL DISTRICT

Aerial view

Mexico City is the largest city
in Mexico, with more than
20 million people. It is divided
into different neighbourhoods
or districts, each with its own
unique features.

ECONOMY
CANADA

Industry

Canada is one of the world's most
economically developed countries.
Computer industries, automotives,
electronics, aeronautics and
chemicals are very important
to the economy. Forests of spruce,
pine and cedar allow the large-
scale manufacturing of paper pulp
and newsprint.

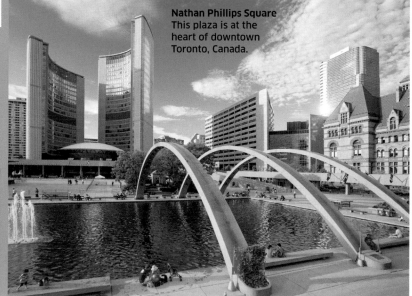

Nathan Phillips Square
This plaza is at the
heart of downtown
Toronto, Canada.

MEXICO CITY

Although it is crowded and has a high level of pollution, Mexico City is steeped in history. The historic centre is built on the ruins of the Aztec capital, and in the elegant district of the Reformation, colonial architecture sits alongside modern buildings.

Country	Mexico
Area	1485 sq km
Population	8,840,000 (city proper)
Density	5952 people per sq km

EMBLEM OF THE CITY

The Angel of Independence

The Angel of Independence was built to honour those who fought against Spanish rule. It was erected in 1910 and was designed by Antonio Rivas Mercado. The monument is located in the Paseo de la Reforma avenue that connects the centre of the city with Chapultepec.

The Winged Victory

The bronze statue (right and below) shows an angel in flight with open arms. In her right hand she holds a wreath.

Burritos

Typical Mexican food includes burritos. Filled with meat and vegetables, these tortilla wraps (below) are served with spicy sauces.

The Cathedral

This is the largest cathedral in Latin America and dominates the main square of Mexico City. The church and its chapels are ornately decorated.

The Zócalo
A view of the main square.

Women's collective
Buses used exclusively by women and children (left) run along the main city streets. There are also different subway lines, buses and trains.

Frida Kahlo Museum
The artist Frida Kahlo lived and died in the neighbourhood of Coyoacan. Today, this house (left) is a museum that exhibits many of her personal items, such as her bed and dresses.

National Palace
The National Palace is an important government building in Mexico. The staircase walls and two courtyard walls are decorated with colourful murals by the Mexican painter Diego Rivera.

THE CITY SQUARE
The Zócalo is one of the largest squares in the world. Flags fly in its centre and on public buildings, restaurants and hotels.

PARKS AND PROMENADES
CHAPULTEPEC AND XOCHIMILCO

Restful places in a busy city
Xochimilco (below) is the only place in Mexico City that still houses the floating gardens (or chinampas), built by the Aztecs.

Chapultepec Park is an enormous green area (bottom) in the middle of this bustling city.

Population
Mexico's constitution recognizes 62 different groups of peoples in the country who have strong links with this region throughout history. This ensures that their culture and language are protected.

THE STATUE OF LIBERTY

One of the world's most famous monuments stands on Liberty Island, south of Manhattan, in New York City. The monument is called 'Liberty Enlightening the World' and was a gift from France to the United States in 1886.

TECHNICAL DESCRIPTION

Opened:
28 October 1886

Location:
Liberty Island,
New York City, USA

Construction:
The figure is made from copper plates. Due to the size and weight of the stone base, it rests on four gigantic steel supports.

IN DETAIL

Support
The statue's strength is created by an internal tower. A skeleton around this tower keeps the outer layer of copper in place.

Plaque
Inside the statue is a plaque with the poem 'The New Colossus' by Emma Lazarus.

Base
The base is square and rests on a star-shaped plinth.

Museums
There are two museums at the foot of the statue.

Head
To reach the head, visitors must climb 354 steps. It is 5 metres from the chin to the skull.

The sculptor

The statue is the work of the French sculptor Frédéric Auguste Bartholdi. An ancient statue, the Colossus of Rhodes, inspired him.

Torch
The torch was originally made from copper, but in 1916, it was changed to 600 pieces of yellow glass to enhance its brightness. The flame is covered with gold leaf.

Manhattan
The statue gives tourists some of the best views of Manhattan Island. With a population of just over 8.1 million, Manhattan is considered one of the largest urban areas in the world.

Crown
There are seven points in the statue's crown. They symbolize the seven seas and the seven continents of the world.

Lift

A lift goes as far as the 10th floor. The 12 further floors must be reached by foot.

Tablet
There is a tablet in the left hand that bears the date of US Independence.

92.99 m

The height of the statue from the base to the torch.

Vision
The statue was the first thing immigrants saw when they arrived by boat in the United States.

Statue
Close-up view of the famous monument.

CENTRAL AMERICA AND THE CARIBBEAN INTRODUCTION

Central America and the Caribbean separate North and South America. The region has areas of volcanic activity as well as places of great natural beauty. The warm tropical climate produces lush vegetation, such as rainforests. The warm, clear waters of the Atlantic Ocean and the Caribbean Sea are home to beautiful coral reefs.

INCREDIBLE HABITAT
THE BELIZE RAINFOREST IS HOME TO THOUSANDS OF SPECIES OF ANIMALS AND PLANTS.

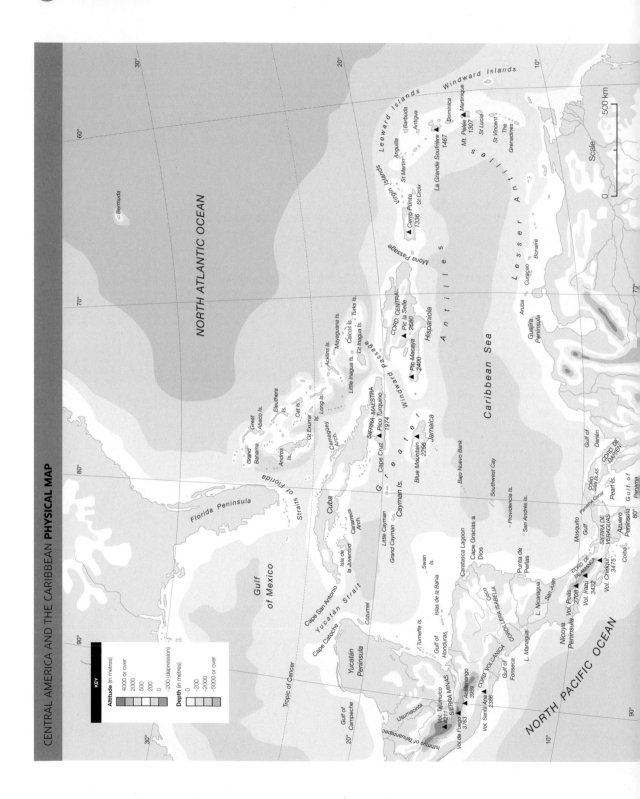

CENTRAL AMERICA AND THE CARIBBEAN **PHYSICAL MAP**

KEY

Altitude (in metres)

4000 or over
2000
500
200
0
-200 (depression)

Depth (in metres)

-200
-2000
-5000 or over

NORTH ATLANTIC OCEAN

Bermuda

Gulf
of Mexico

Florida Peninsula

Straits of Florida

Gulf of
Campeche

Tropic of Cancer

Yucatán
Peninsula

Cape Catoche

Cape San Antonio

Yucatán Strait

Cozumel

Isthmus of Tehuantepec

Usumacinta

Vol. Tajumulco
4211
SIERRA MINAS
Acatenango
3959
Vol. de Fuego
3763
Vol. Santa Ana
2386
CORD. VOLCANICA

Gulf of
Honduras

Islas de la Bahía

Swan
Is.

Turneffe Is.

Cuba

Isla de
la Juventud

Canarreos
Arch.

Little Cayman
Grand Cayman
Cayman Is.

Gulf of
Fonseca

L. Managua
L. Nicaragua

CORDILLERA ISABELIA

Caratasca Lagoon

Cape Gracias a
Dios

Punta de
Perlas

Providencia Is.

San Andrés Is.

Southwest Cay

Bajo Nuevo Bank

Mosquito
Gulf

Nicoya
Peninsula

Vol. Poás
2708
Vol. Irazú
3432
CORD DE
TALAMANCA
Vol. Chirripó
3475

Coco

San Juan

Azuero
Peninsula

SIERRA DE
VERAGUAS

Panama Canal

CORD
SAN BLAS

Gulf of
Panama

Coiba

Pearl Is.

CORD. DE
DARIEN

Gulf of
Darién

NORTH PACIFIC OCEAN

Great
Bahama

Grand
Bahama

Abaco Is.

Andros
Is.

Eleuthera
Is.

Cat Is.

Gt Exuma
Is.

Long Is.

Camagüey
Arch.

Acklins Is.

Mayaguana Is.

Little Inagua Is.
Gt Inagua Is.

Caicos Is.
Turks Is.

Cape Cruz
SIERRA MAESTRA
Pico Turquino
1974

Blue Mountain
2256
Jamaica

Greater
Antilles

Windward Passage

Mona Passage

CORD CENTRAL
Pic la Selle
2680
Pic Macaya
2400
Hispaniola

Caribbean Sea

Virgin Islands
St Croix
Cerro Punta
1336

Anguilla
St Martin
Barbuda
Antigua

Leeward Islands

La Grande Soufrière
1467

Dominica

Mt. Pelée
1307
Martinique
St Lucia
St Vincent
The
Grenadines

Windward Islands

Lesser Antilles

Aruba
Curaçao
Bonaire

Guajira
Peninsula

90°   30°
20°
Tropic of Cancer
80°
70°
60°
30°
20°
10°
90°
10°
70°

500 km

Scale

0

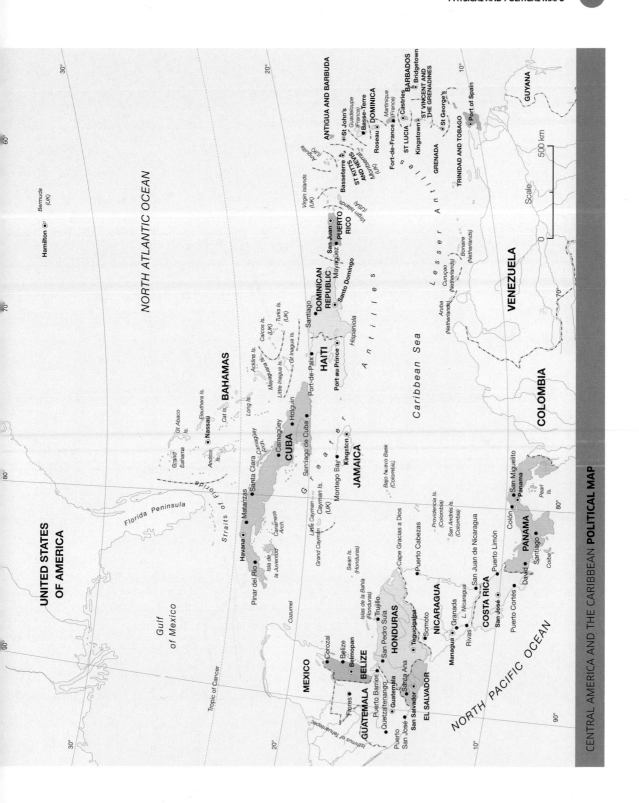

CENTRAL AMERICA AND THE CARIBBEAN **POLITICAL MAP**

UNITED STATES
OF AMERICA

NORTH ATLANTIC OCEAN

Bermuda
(UK)
Hamilton

Gulf
of Mexico

Florida Peninsula

Tropic of Cancer

Straits of Florida

MEXICO

Cozumel

Isthmus of Tehuantepec

GUATEMALA

Flores
Puerto
Barrios
San José
Quetzaltenango
Guatemala
Santa Ana
San Salvador

EL SALVADOR

Corozal
Belize
Belmopan

BELIZE

San Pedro Sula
Trujillo
Islas de la Bahía
(Honduras)
Swan Is.
(Honduras)

HONDURAS

Tegucigalpa
Somoto

Cape Gracias a Dios

Puerto Cabezas

NICARAGUA

Managua
Granada
L. Nicaragua
Rivas
San Juan de Nicaragua
Puerto Limón

San José

COSTA RICA

David
Santiago
Colba

PANAMA

San Miguelito
Panama
Colón

Pearl
Is.

Providencia Is.
(Colombia)
San Andrés Is.
(Colombia)

Bajo Nuevo Bank
(Colombia)

NORTH PACIFIC OCEAN

BAHAMAS

Grand
Bahama
Is.
Gt Abaco
Is.
Eleuthera Is.
Cat Is.
Nassau
Andros
Is.
Long Is.

Camagüey
Arch.

Havana
Matanzas
Pinar del Rio
Santa Clara
Camagüey
Holguin

CUBA

Isla de
la Juventud
Canarreos
Arch.
Cayman Is.
(UK)
Little Cayman
Grand Cayman

Santiago de Cuba

Acklins Is.
Mayaguana Is.
Little Inagua Is.
Gt Inagua Is.

Caicos Is.
Turks Is.
(UK)

Greater Antilles

JAMAICA

Montego Bay
Kingston

Caribbean Sea

Santiago
Port-de-Paix
Port au Prince

HAITI

Hispaniola

DOMINICAN
REPUBLIC

Santo Domingo

Mayagüez
San Juan
PUERTO
RICO

Virgin Islands
(UK)
Virgin Islands
(USA)

Anguilla
(UK)

ANTIGUA AND BARBUDA
St John's

Basseterre
ST KITTS
AND NEVIS
Montserrat
(UK)

Guadeloupe
(France)
Basse-Terre

Roseau
DOMINICA

Martinique
(France)
Fort-de-France

ST LUCIA
Castries

BARBADOS
Bridgetown

ST VINCENT AND
THE GRENADINES
Kingstown

GRENADA
St George's

TRINIDAD AND TOBAGO
Port of Spain

Lesser Antilles

Aruba
(Netherlands)
Curaçao
(Netherlands)
Bonaire
(Netherlands)

COLOMBIA

VENEZUELA

GUYANA

Scale

0
500 km

30°
20°
10°

60°
70°
80°
90°

30°
20°
10°

80°
90°
70°

FLORA AND FAUNA

Mountains, sea-washed shores and tropical rainforests are found throughout Central America and the Caribbean. The region's plants and animals are very varied. Alligators, iguanas and coral reefs are all found here.

Kinkajou

The kinkajou, also known as the honey bear, lives in Central America. It is a nocturnal mammal that lives in trees and feeds on fruits.

Jaguar

The jaguar (left) is the largest carnivore in the Americas and one of the largest worldwide. This cat is in danger of extinction.

Macaw

The red-and-green macaw (left) nests in hollow trees in the region's forests. It feeds on seeds and fruit.

Quetzal

With its brightly-coloured feathers and long tail, the quetzal is the national bird of Guatemala.

Reptiles

The green iguana lives in areas of thick vegetation where there is an average annual temperature of 28 °C.

Guatemala
Semuc Champey is a beautiful lake on the River Cahabón in Guatemala.

Silvertip shark

The silvertip shark is found in the Pacific Ocean. It reaches a maximum length of 3 metres. It is a danger to humans.

Forest ruins

The Tikal National Park is found in the Petén region of Guatemala. The park is home to pumas, jaguars, birds such as toucans and parrots, and many species of monkey. Tikal was once one of the biggest cities of the Mayan civilization. The ruins of the city lie in the park.

**COLOURFUL
MARINE LIFE**

Coral reefs in Belize

Beautiful coral reefs lie just off the shore of Belize. The reefs are about 300 kilometres long. They are the second largest in the world, after the Great Barrier Reef in Australia. These reefs are home to many different species of fish.

POPULATION AND ECONOMY

Much of the population of Central America and the Caribbean is descended from Africans, Europeans and Asians. The economies of most of the countries are based on tourism and agriculture. Bananas, cotton, sugar cane and tobacco are some of the most widely-grown crops.

Haiti
Street vendors in Haiti sell fruit and vegetables.

Bananas
Many different fruit are grown for export. There is a high demand for bananas exported from the region.

Tobacco
One of the world's most valuable crops, tobacco is grown in Cuba, Guatemala, Nicaragua, the Dominican Republic and Honduras.

Sugar cane
The region produces large amounts of sugar cane. It is usually harvested by hand, providing work for many people.

Dominican Republic
This is a typical fishing village located on the northwest coast.

MAIN ETHNIC GROUPS

African heritage

African influences can be seen in many aspects of daily life in the region. For example, there is music that has developed from African traditions, such as the mambo. Many of the people also hold spiritual beliefs that are based on African religions.

Junkanoo
On this holiday in the Bahamas, the biggest parade takes place in Nassau.

EVERYDAY LIFE
GENDER ROLES

Role of women

In this region, women often have to work harder than men. Recent studies confirm that women spend more time in unpaid activities than men.

LOSS OF CROPS
HEAVY RAINS

Honduras

In 2010, heavy rains fell across Honduras. This caused landslides that destroyed many homes and ruined many of the crops.

THE PANAMA CANAL

A work of engineering brilliance, the Panama Canal allows ships to move between the Atlantic and Pacific oceans without going around South America. The first ship passed through the canal in 1914. In 2007, building began on an extension of the canal.

LAKE

CHAMBER

CHAMBER

Ocean to ocean

It is approx. 80 kilometres from one ocean to the other, travelling through the Panama Canal.

There and back

There are two parallel channels, one for raising the water level and the other for lowering it.

CHAMBER

The lake

At the centre of the canal is a lake, which is 26 metres above sea level. Its water fills the locks.

CHAMBER

Building works

Currently, 14,000 ships cross the canal each year. Once the building works are completed, 18,000 ships will pass through the canal every year.

How the locks work

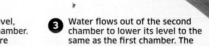

1 The water in the first lock chamber must be at sea level. To reach sea level, it releases 378 million litres of fresh water in just eight minutes.

2 When its water is at sea level, the ship enters the first chamber. The valves and dampers are then closed and the water is returned to the lock to raise the water level.

3 Water flows out of the second chamber to lower its level to the same as the first chamber. The ship passes into the second chamber, and the process is repeated for the third chamber.

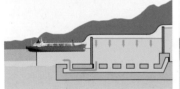

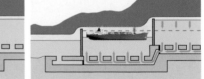

8–10 hours

The average time taken to travel through the canal by boat.

THE NEW CANAL
WORK BEGAN IN 2007

Large ships

For decades, most of the world's cargo was carried on ships that were specifically built to travel through the canal. However, many of today's ships are now too large to pass through the canal.

Giant locks

Two new locks (positioned next to the current canal) will make it possible for these larger ships to travel through the canal. The new canal will also have a system of pools to save fresh water.

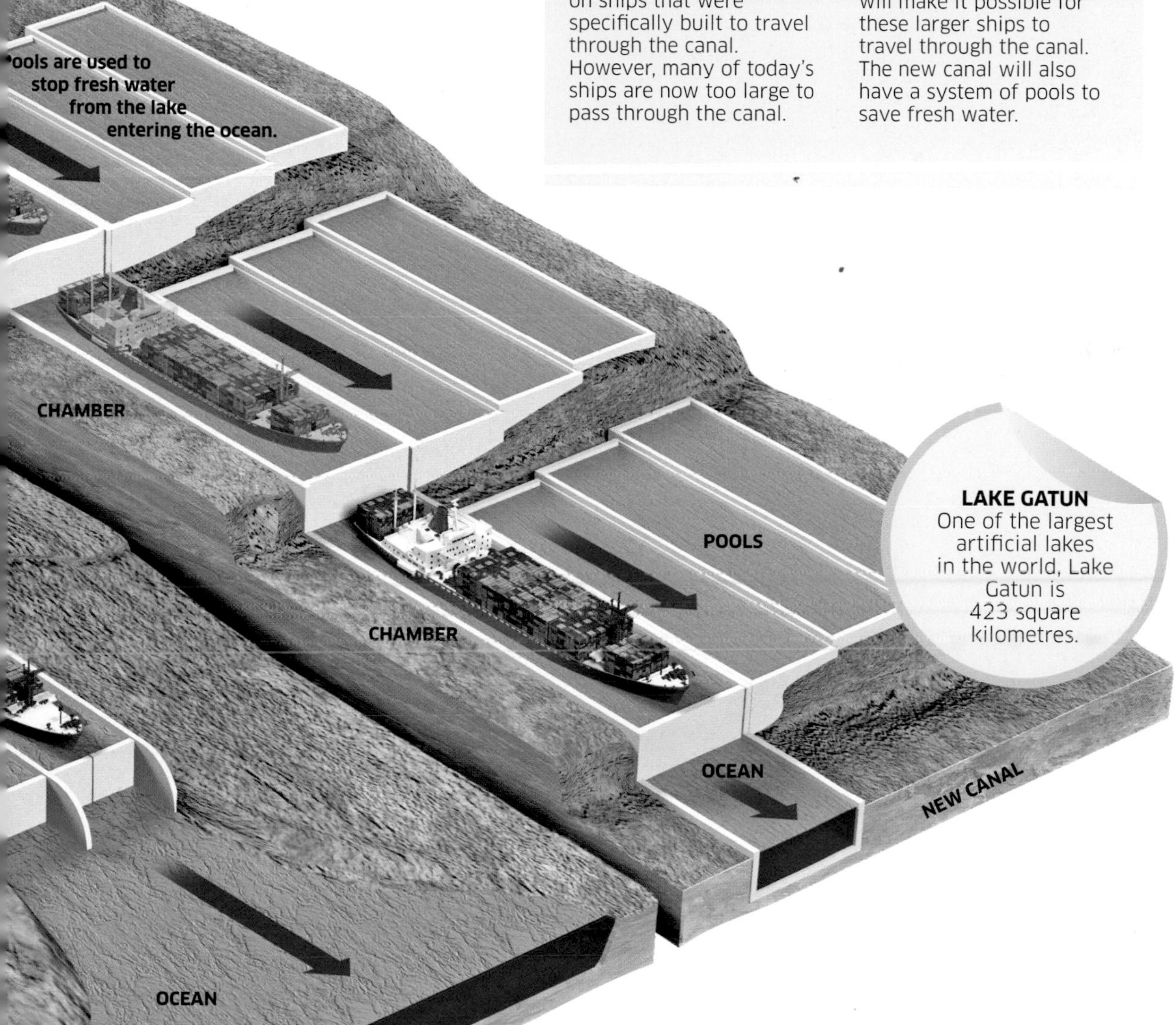

'ools are used to stop fresh water from the lake entering the ocean.
CHAMBER
POOLS
CHAMBER
LAKE GATUN
One of the largest artificial lakes in the world, Lake Gatun is 423 square kilometres.
OCEAN
NEW CANAL
OCEAN
CURRENT CANAL

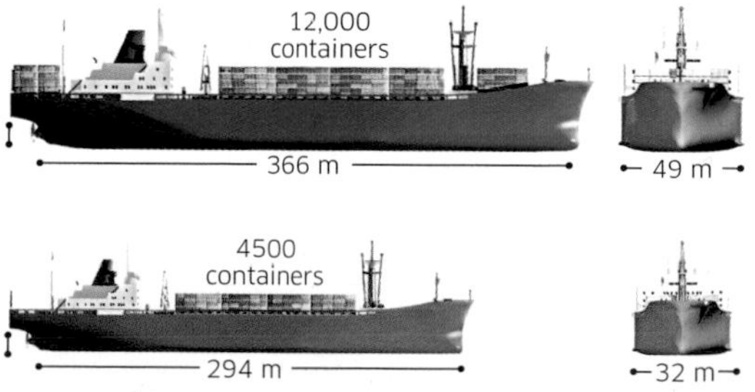

Ship fitting new canal
Depth: 15 m
12,000 containers
366 m
49 m
Ship fitting old canal
Depth: 12 m
4500 containers
294 m
32 m

SOUTH AMERICA INTRODUCTION

This large continent extends from the northern hemisphere down close to the Antarctic Circle. It has a huge range of climates, from tropical rainforest and hot desert, to the dry cold of Patagonia in southern Argentina. Most of the continent forms part of an area called Latin America, which is made up of the former colonies of Spain and Portugal. For this reason, Spanish and Portuguese are the most widely spoken languages. There are also a large number of other languages and cultures on the continent. In the Amazon Rainforest, there are still a few small groups of people who have never contacted the outside world.

THICK CLOUDS
THE ANDES MOUNTAINS RUN ALONG THE WEST OF THE CONTINENT, PARALLEL TO THE PACIFIC COAST.

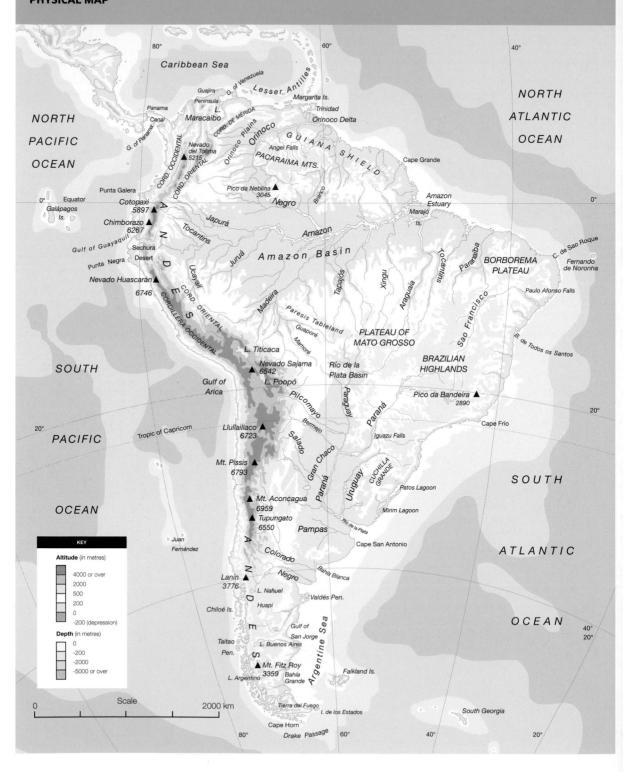

SOUTH AMERICA
PHYSICAL MAP

NORTH
PACIFIC
OCEAN

Caribbean Sea

Guajira
Peninsula
Panama
Canal
G. of Panama
L.
Maracaibo
CORD. DE MÉRIDA

G. of Venezuela
Lesser Antilles
Margarita Is.
Trinidad
Orinoco Delta

NORTH
ATLANTIC
OCEAN

CORD. OCCIDENTAL
CORD. ORIENTAL
Nevado
del Tolima
5215

Orinoco Plains
Orinoco
PACARAIMA MTS.
Angel Falls
GUIANA SHIELD
Cape Grande

Punta Galera
0°   Equator
Galápagos
Is.
Cotopaxi
5897
Chimborazo
6267
A
N
D

Japurá
Negro
Branco
Pico da Neblina
3045
Negro

Amazon
Estuary
Marajó
Is.

0°

Gulf of Guayaquil
Sechura
Desert
Punta Negra
E
S
Tocantins
Ucayali
Juruá
Amazon
Amazon Basin

C. de Sao Roque
Fernando
de Noronha

Nevado Huascarán
6746
CORD. ORIENTAL
CORDILLERA OCCIDENTAL
Madeira
Paresis Tableland
Guaporé
Tapajós
Xingu
Araguaia
Tocantins
Paranaíba
São Francisco
BORBOREMA
PLATEAU
Paulo Afonso Falls
B. de Todos os Santos

SOUTH

PACIFIC

OCEAN

L. Titicaca
Nevado Sajama
6542
L. Poopó
Mamoré
PLATEAU OF
MATO GROSSO
BRAZILIAN
HIGHLANDS

Gulf of
Arica
Río de la
Plata Basin
Pilcomayo
Pico da Bandeira
2890

20°

20°
Tropic of Capricorn
Llullaillaco
6723
Bermejo
Paraguay
Paraná
Iguazu Falls
Cape Frío

SOUTH

Mt. Pissis
6793
Salado
Gran Chaco
Paraná
Uruguay
CUCHILLA GRANDE
Patos Lagoon
ATLANTIC

Mt. Aconcagua
6959
Tupungato
6550
A
N
Pampas
Mirim Lagoon
Río de la Plata
Cape San Antonio

Juan
Fernández
Colorado
Negro
Bahía Blanca

OCEAN

40°
20°

Lanín
3776
D
L. Nahuel
Huapi
Valdés Pen.

Chiloé Is.
E
Gulf of
San Jorge
S
Argentine Sea

Taitao
Pen.
L. Buenos Aires
Falkland Is.

Mt. Fitz Roy
3359
Bahía
Grande
L. Argentino
Tierra del Fuego
I. de los Estados
South Georgia

Cape Horn
Drake Passage

KEY

Altitude (in metres)

4000 or over
2000
500
200
0
-200 (depression)

Depth (in metres)

0
-200
-2000
-5000 or over

0   Scale   2000 km

80°   60°   40°   20°

SOUTH AMERICA
POLITICAL MAP

NORTH
PACIFIC
OCEAN

NORTH
ATLANTIC
OCEAN

Lesser Antilles

Barranquilla
Maracaibo
Margarita Is.
(Ven.)
Caracas
Trinidad
Valencia

VENEZUELA

Georgetown
Medellín
Paramaribo
GUYANA
Cali
Cayenne
Bogotá
SURINAME
COLOMBIA
FRENCH
GUIANA

0°
Galápagos Is.
(Ecuador)
Equator
0°

Quito
ECUADOR
Guayaquil
Manaus
Belém
São Luís
Fortaleza
Fernando
de Noronha
(Brazil)

Chiclayo
B R A Z I L
Natal
Recife
Maceió

PERU

Lima
Salvador

BOLIVIA
La Paz
Brasília
Arequipa
Cochabamba

S O U T H
Sucre
Belo Horizonte

PARAGUAY
Rio de Janeiro
20°
20°

P A C I F I C
Antofagasta
Salta
Asunción
São Paulo
Tropic of Capricorn
Ciudad del Este

CHILE
San Miguel
de Tucumán
Florianópolis

O C E A N
Santa Fe
Porto Alegre
Córdoba
Salto
Valparaíso
URUGUAY
S O U T H
Santiago de Chile
Buenos Aires
Montevideo
La Plata
Juan
Fernández
(Chile)
ARGENTINA
A T L A N T I C
Bahía Blanca

Valdivia
Viedma

Chiloé Is.
Rawson
O C E A N
40°
20°
40°
Comodoro Rivadavia

100°
Falkland Is.
(UK)

0
Scale
2000 km
South
Georgia
(UK)
Río Gallegos

80°
60°
40°
20°

FLORA AND FAUNA

South America boasts a wide range of landscapes and environments. In the tropical forests, there is a rich diversity of animal and plant life, while very different organisms survive in the cold south, or high in the Andes Mountains.

Water lilies in the Wetlands of Pantanal, Brazil.

AMAZON BASIN

Abundance of life

The largest rainforest in the world lies around the giant River Amazon. More species of animal and plant live here than anywhere else on the planet. The Amazon is the second-longest river in the world, but the largest in terms of volume of water. It contains 20 per cent of all the river water in the world.

DESERT SCRUB ANDES – PATAGONIA

Tough species

This dry environment extends from Colombia in the north to Argentina in the south. It follows the Andes Mountains and includes regions of high plateau and the coastal deserts of Chile and Peru. Vegetation is mostly grassland. The animals living here have adapted to survive in tough conditions.

DIVERSITY THE ANDES MOUNTAINS

High living

The mountain landscape includes dry areas with sparse vegetation and forested areas, such as the Yungas in Bolivia. Many different species of tree grow in the mountain forests. The condor, the Andean flamingo and the guanaco (a large mammal similar to a camel) can be found in the Andes.

Buzzard-eagle
This bird of prey has special feathers that stop it from freezing to death when it flies over the Andes.

Guianan cock-of-the-rock
This beautiful bird lives in high rocky areas. It feeds mainly on fruit.

FINE WOOL
Alpacas grow high-quality wool, which is excellent for knitting warm clothing.

Alpaca
The alpaca is very common on the high plains of Ecuador, Bolivia, Chile and Peru.

Carnivore
The leopard seal is one of the largest predators in the Southern Ocean.

Snake
The red-tailed boa lives in northern South America.

Piranhas
There are several species of piranha in the River Amazon. These carnivorous fish can sometimes come together into large schools to attack their prey. However, they rarely attack humans.

Patagonian woods
Larch, myrtle and monkey puzzle (above, from left to right) are three of the trees found in Patagonia. Below are the most common plant species that grow there:

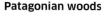

1. Verbena
2. Antarctic beech
3. Larch
4. Myrtle
5. Lenga beech
6. Monkey puzzle
7. Hazel

Iguanas and crabs
The Barrington land iguana (left) and infered rock crab (below) both live on the Galapagos Islands.

CRISIS IN THE AMAZON

One-fifth of the Amazon Rainforest has been cut down by humans since 1970. However, there are encouraging signs that the rate of destruction is slowing down as the governments of Brazil and other countries take action. Further destruction of the Amazon could damage the whole world's climate.

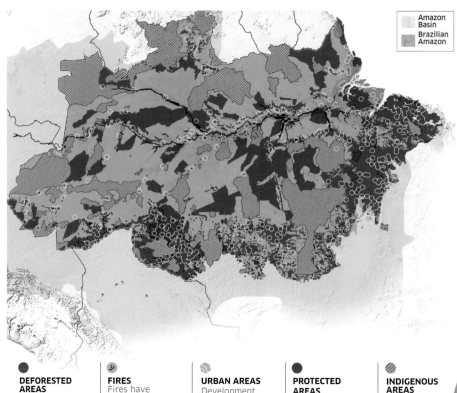

Amazon Basin

Brazilian Amazon

 DEFORESTED AREAS
In these areas, all the trees have been cut down.

 FIRES
Fires have been used to clear land for agriculture.

 URBAN AREAS
Development of urban areas is unplanned and growing.

PROTECTED AREAS
National parks that cannot be cut down.

 INDIGENOUS AREAS
These areas have some protection.

WHAT IS AT STAKE?
ISSUES THAT AFFECT US ALL

Oxygen
Plants in the Amazon produce about 20 per cent of the oxygen on Earth. They act like the 'lungs of the planet'.

Greenhouse effect
Trees absorb carbon dioxide from the air, slowing down global warming. Without the rainforest, the planet will get hotter more quickly.

Biodiversity
An estimated 10 per cent of all the known species of plant and animal live in the Amazon Basin.

Culture
It is thought that about 200,000 indigenous people live in the area. Their diverse cultures could be lost.

AMAZON BASIN
MANY COUNTRIES

A huge area

The Amazon Basin extends across an area of about 7 million square kilometres crossing several countries. Half of the rainforest lies in Brazil. The rest is spread across Peru, Bolivia, Colombia, Venezuela, Guyana and Suriname.

Rate of loss

By 1991, the Amazon had lost 415,000 square kilometres of forest. By 2000, that number had risen to 587,000 square kilometres. The cleared land is used to graze livestock and to grow crops. The rate of loss has been slowing in recent years.

Aerial view
The River Amazon empties approximately 200,000 cubic metres of water into the ocean every second.

People in danger

Many small groups of people call the Amazon home, such as the Yanomami (pictured left). These groups are in danger of losing their way of life, and with it, a huge amount of knowledge about the forest and its plants will be lost.

Rubber

Rubber trees are grown along the banks of the River Tapajos in Brazil. The rubber is collected from cuts made in the bark.

POPULATION

Many people across South America are moving from the countryside to the cities. This has caused rapid and disorganized growth as makeshift homes are built on the outskirts of large cities. These poor urban areas are known as favelas, or shantytowns.

Rio de Janeiro
A view of this Brazilian city, home to more than 6 million people.

BRAZIL
PORTO ALEGRE

Skyscrapers and motorways

Porto Alegre is the capital city of the state of Rio Grande do Sul. It has a population of nearly 1.5 million and is a centre for industry and business.

Salvador da Bahia

The first capital city of Portugal's New World Empire, Salvador was founded in 1549. It is one of the oldest cities in Brazil. The historic city centre has been made a UNESCO World Heritage Site. It has a population of about 3 million people.

Carnival

In Brazil, the biggest and most important festival is called Carnival. People take to the streets in ornate costumes to have a huge party.

VENEZUELA
CARACAS

Booming city

With a population of more than 3.5 million inhabitants, Caracas is the ninth-largest urban area in Latin America. It is a commercial centre that sees a lot of investment from Venezuelan companies and also from abroad.

COLOMBIA
BOGOTA

Cultural centre

Colombia's main museums and most important universities are found in its capital city, Bogota. It has a population of more than 6.5 million people. Below is an image of the historic Church of St Francis in the city.

La Boca
A suburb of the city of Buenos Aires, the capital of Argentina.

ARGENTINA
CORDOBA

Second city

The second-largest city in Argentina after Buenos Aires, Cordoba has a population of 1.3 million people. It is known as 'the learned one' because the country's best university is found there. Below is the city's cathedral.

Mate
A popular drink in Argentina.

CHILE
SANTIAGO DE CHILE

High life expectancy

With a population of more than 5 million people, Chile's capital city, Santiago, is the largest city in the country. The city contains a rich mix of fine old and striking new architecture. Chile is the country with the longest life expectancy in South America, at around 79 years.

ECONOMIC RESOURCES

South America produces a lot of food for export to other parts of the world. It also has many natural resources and some of the largest oil reserves on the planet. Brazil has the largest economy in South America, followed by Argentina, Colombia, Venezuela, Peru and Chile.

ARGENTINA
TOURISM

Favourite destination

The Perito Moreno Glacier is a popular tourist attraction. The drive to the glacier from El Calafate takes in a series of lakes, streams, woods and snow-capped mountains.

Wonder
The huge glacier is a spectacular natural wonder.

VENEZUELA
OIL

Important reserve

Oil is the main source of income in Venezuela. Today, a state-owned company manages the country's reserves, which are among the largest in the world. As of January 2011, it had 297 billion barrels left (1 barrel = 159 litres). In 1960, Venezuela was one of the founding members of OPEC, an association of oil producers around the world. It also has reserves of natural gas, methane, iron, gold and diamonds. Venezuelan industry concentrates on oil refinery and petrochemicals, which are chemicals made using oil. Its exports are mainly products made from oil or steel. It also has textile, timber and pharmaceutical industries.

URUGUAY
AGRICULTURE AND TOURISM

Sunflowers

The second-smallest country in South America, Uruguay is known for its fine beaches, such as Punta del Este. Its economy is based around cattle farming and other agriculture. Among the crops grown are soya, wheat, barley, oats, rice, maize and sunflowers (below).

Maracaibo
A centre for
oil production.

CHILE
MINING

Taking full advantage

Mining is the most important industry in Chile, in particular copper mining, which is very profitable. Pictured left is the Chuquicamata mine in the Atacama Desert. Wine-making is another important industry, and Chile exports wine around the world. A typical Chilean vineyard is shown below.

Chuquicamata This is an open-cast mine.

BRAZIL AND COLOMBIA
COFFEE AND MUCH MORE

Powerful economies

Brazil has traditionally been a large producer of coffee. However, a growing financial sector means that the service sector is now the largest part of the economy, followed by industry. Colombia is still a large producer and exporter of coffee.

Exploitation The Amazon has lost much of its forests, cut down to make way for human activity.

BOLIVIA
ABUNDANT NATURAL GAS

Source of energy

Bolivia has the second-largest reserves of natural gas in South America. It exports the gas to its neighbours, in particular Brazil and Argentina. It also has smaller oil reserves and many different minerals are mined. The picture below shows some typical gas tankers.

THE NAZCA LINES

The Nazca Lines are drawings on the land in south Peru, some of them more than 300 metres long. They are line drawings of animals, plants and geometric shapes, which can be seen only from a great height. The lines were drawn on the plain and on the hillsides by the Nazca people, who lived there between 200 BC and AD 500.

PERU
NAZCA

Location

The lines are found in the provinces of Palpa and Nazca on the Pampas de Jumana.

COLOMBIA
ECUADOR
PERU
BRAZIL
Lima
Cusco
PACIFIC
OCEAN
Nazca
Arequipa
BOLIVIA

World Heritage Site

In 1994, UNESCO declared the drawings a World Heritage Site.

Entry and exit

The Spider has an entrance and an exit, which allow you to follow the lines without ever crossing from one line to another.

Strange features

The shape and features of the Spider show that it is based on a species from the Amazon Rainforest.

The Spider
One of the best-known figures, the Spider, is made from one continuous line.

Anthony F. Aveni

A scientist from the USA, Aveni linked the lines to water supplies. He believed that they were used in rituals to secure water for crops.

LEGACY OF THE NAZCA

Cultural works
The Nazca were fine craftspeople. They made good cloths and their pottery was the best in pre-Colombian South America.

Head-trophy
This trophy was found in a tomb.

Two-headed snake
A sacred symbol commonly found in the Andes.

Siku
The Siku is a traditional Andean musical instrument.

Cemetery
Nearby, there is a cemetery dating from pre-Colombian times. This mummy was found there.

Map of the stars
Some researchers, such as Maria Reiche, have suggested that the Spider is a representation of the star formation Orion.

The ground
The surface is covered with a layer of dark reddish stones.

The Spider
Viewed from the air.

BUENOS AIRES

A fascinating city, Buenos Aires is the most densely populated city in Argentina. In the centre of the city there are many historical buildings next to the River Plate. At Puerto Madero nearby, there are stunningly modern developments.

SYMBOLS OF THE CITY

The Teatro Colón

This magnificent concert hall has some of the best acoustics in the world. This means that the audience can hear the music clearly.

Avenida 9 de Julio

At 140 metres wide, this is one of the widest streets in the world. The Obelisk, a famous monument, stands at the junction with Corrientes Avenue.

Town hall

This building has stood for nearly all of the country's 200 years of independence.

The Frigate Sarmiento

This ship from the Argentinian navy saw service between 1898 and 1961. Today, it is a museum.

Country	Argentina
Area	202 sq km
Population	2,891,082
Density	14,314 people/sq km

Night scene
Puerto Madero has striking new developments, restaurants and homes.

Puerto Madero

The old port area has seen massive development, with a new residential district and a business centre.

NAME
Puerto Madero is named after Eduardo Madero, who drew up the original plans for the port in 1882.

CULTURE IN BUENOS AIRES

Museums

The city has a wide range of museums, including the Proa (top), the Malba (bottom), the Museum of the Fine Arts and the Museum of Modern Art.

Lezama Park

This park was once a farm owned by the Lezama family. It contains a wide range of different trees, winding paths, a large pergola, waterfalls, monuments, stairways and an amphitheatre.

Underground

The city's underground railway system has six lines. The first station opened in 1913. It was the first underground to be built in South America and is one of the busiest in the world.

CHRIST THE REDEEMER

The majestic statue of Christ the Redeemer stands with arms outstretched over the centre of Rio de Janeiro in Brazil. It is built on the rocky summit of Mount Corcovado, 709 metres above sea level. It is surrounded by the Tijuca Forest, the largest area of urban woodland in the world.

CHRIST THE REDEEMER
FACT FILE

Height:
38 metres

Outer covering:
Greenish-grey soapstone

Weight:
635 tonnes

Interior:
The structure is made of hollow
reinforced concrete

CULTURAL AND RELIGIOUS WORK

Historical facts

The statue took nine years to build and was opened on 12 October 1931. It was a technical challenge because the area is very windy, and it was very difficult to build the outstretched arms and the bent head. The project was run by the engineer Heitor da Silva Costa. The artist Carlos Oswald came up with the final design, while the sculptor Paul Landowski (below) made the head and the hands.

Coating
Soapstone from Minas Gerais was chosen because bad weather and changes in temperature do not damage it.

Church
At the foot of the statue is a small church.

Height
From the base
to the head it is
38 metres, including
the 8-metre plinth.

2003
The year that
escalators were
installed to carry
people to the base
of the statue.

Symbol
The imposing statue
is one of the largest
religious images in
the world and has
become a symbol
of Brazil.

Head
The head is bent
downwards slightly.

Interior
Contains beams
and staircases.

Arms
Each arm is
27 metres long.

Mountain train
The Corcovado Railway
was opened in 1884.
Trains climb through
the lush Tijuca Forest at
a steady 12 km/h. The
trains carried the pieces
of the statue up to the
top of the mountain.

THE AMERICAS

GEOGRAPHICAL WONDERS

Mountains, high plateaus, vast plains, deserts, jungles, volcanoes and glaciers: North, Central and South America offer a series of spectacular and varied landscapes. There are also large areas of land that are still untouched by humans, many of them now protected as World Heritage Sites.

ALBERTA
CANADA

Banff National Park

Bow Lake in Banff National Park, Alberta, freezes over every winter. Covering an area of 6641 square kilometres, the park is home to glaciers, woods and mountains. UNESCO has declared the park a World Heritage Site.

Glacier landscape
Tyre tracks run over the surface of a frozen lake near the Canadian Rockies.

CANADA TO NEW MEXICO
UNITED STATES

The Rocky Mountains

This mountain range extends for more than 4800 kilometres from northern Canada to New Mexico in the south. A young mountain range, it was formed from a series of separate mountain chains that joined together. Between the peaks, the valleys are home to spectacular forests and lakes.

CALIFORNIA
UNITED STATES

San Andreas Fault

The North American and Pacific tectonic plates collide at the San Andreas Fault, which runs parallel to the coast of California and through the city of San Francisco. It is a very unstable area, prone to devastating earthquakes.

CANADA
NORTH AMERICA

Canadian Shield

The Canadian Shield is an ancient chain of eroded mountains that runs alongside Hudson Bay. It forms the shape of a huge horseshoe and has an average height of 300 metres.

CENTRAL AMERICA AND THE CARIBBEAN

Irazu Volcano

With a height of 3432 metres, Irazu is the highest active volcano in Costa Rica. The summit has five craters. One of the craters is filled with a green lake (left).

Sierra Maestra

Surrounded by lush vegetation, the Sierra Maestra is a mountain chain in southeastern Cuba. Pico Turquino is the highest peak in the Sierra Maestra, reaching 1974 metres above sea level.

Punta Cana
An area of beautiful beaches on the east coast of the Dominican Republic.

SOUTH AMERICA
AMAZON BASIN

The great river

The Amazon is the largest river in the world (by volume of water). About 200 smaller rivers flow into it emptying it into the Atlantic Ocean through a huge delta. From the Andes, it flows 6737 kilometres across South America.

Atacama Desert

The Atacama is one of the driest places on the planet. It extends through the north of Chile between the River Copiapo and the River Loa. Parts of the desert contain rock formations that look like the surface of the Moon.

ARGENTINA
EL CALAFATE

Perito Moreno Glacier

Measuring 30 kilometres long and 5 kilometres wide, the Perito Moreno Glacier is found in the province of Santa Cruz. Every now and then, there are spectacular crashes of ice as large chunks fall off the front of the glacier.

PEOPLE AND LANGUAGES

Spanish and English are the most widely-spoken languages in the Americas. French and Portuguese are also spoken, as are a wide range of indigenous languages, such as Quechua, Guarani and Mapuche.

Spanish

Spanish was introduced by the Conquistadors. Since then, the language of each region has changed, developing its own vocabulary and accent.

ORIGINS
The population of the Americas is descended mainly from Amerindians, Africans and Europeans.

English
The main language of science, trade and diplomacy.

Culture
Many smaller cultures across the world are in danger of disappearing. Along with them, their languages are lost.

Saving languages
Anthropologists believe that it is vital to save languages because they give us different ways of seeing the world.

ORIGINAL LANGUAGES OF THE AMERICAS

Canada and the United States
There are more than 300 native languages but many are in the process of dying out.

1. Algonquian-Ritwan
2. Caddo
3. Hokan
4. Iroquois
5. Kiowa-Tano
6. Muskogee
7. Others

Mexico and Central America
Quiche and Yucatec are Mayan languages that are still spoken. Many others have disappeared.

1. Macro-Chibcha
2. Maya
3. Mixe-Zoque
4. Oto-Manguean
5. Totonac
6. Uto-Aztecan
7. Others

South America
More than 1000 languages have died out. Some, such as Quechua, are still spoken.

1. Arawak
2. Carib
3. Macro-Chibcha
4. Macro-Ge
5. Pano-Tacanan
6. Quechumaran
7. Others

MAIN NATIVE LANGUAGES
IMPORTANT FACTS

PERU
QUECHUA

Widely-spoken language
Peru has a great ethnic diversity. Quechua, the language spoken by the Incas, is the language most spoken. It is also spoken in Bolivia, Ecuador, Colombia, Argentina and Chile.

MEXICO
NAHUATL

A range of languages
In Mexico, about 6 million people speak a range of more than 60 native languages. Nahuatl, the Mayan languages and Zapotec are the most common.

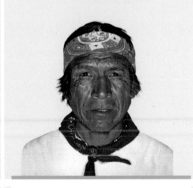

CHILE
MAPUCHE

Influence
The Mapuche, also known as the Araucanians, live in southern Chile and southwest Argentina. Many of their neighbours adopted their language.

CARIBBEAN
CREOLE

African roots
In Haiti and Dominique, most people speak Creole, which is a language that mixes French vocabulary with the grammar of West African languages.

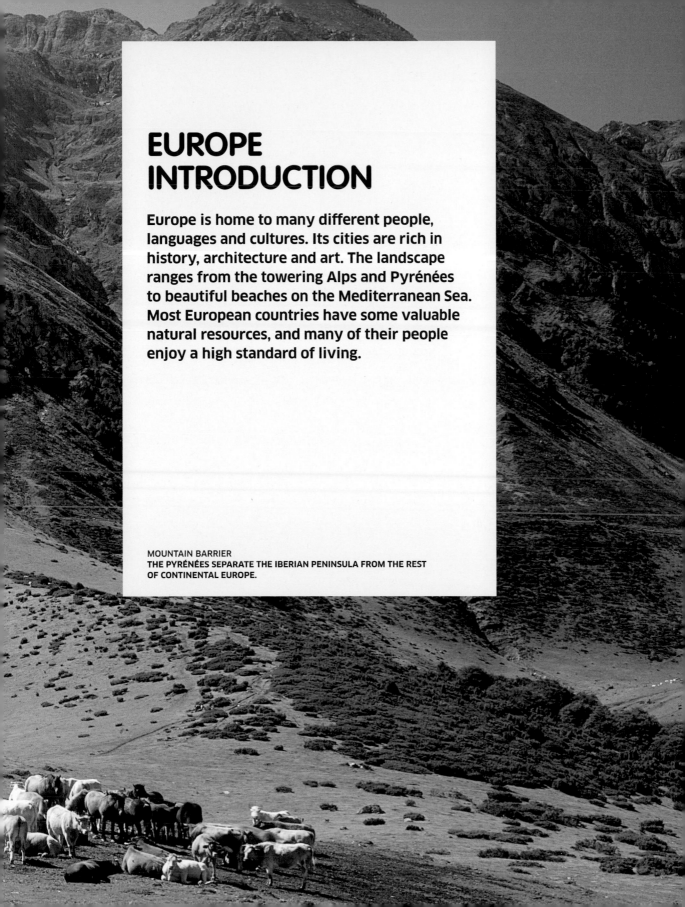

EUROPE INTRODUCTION

Europe is home to many different people, languages and cultures. Its cities are rich in history, architecture and art. The landscape ranges from the towering Alps and Pyrénées to beautiful beaches on the Mediterranean Sea. Most European countries have some valuable natural resources, and many of their people enjoy a high standard of living.

MOUNTAIN BARRIER
THE PYRÉNÉES SEPARATE THE IBERIAN PENINSULA FROM THE REST OF CONTINENTAL EUROPE.

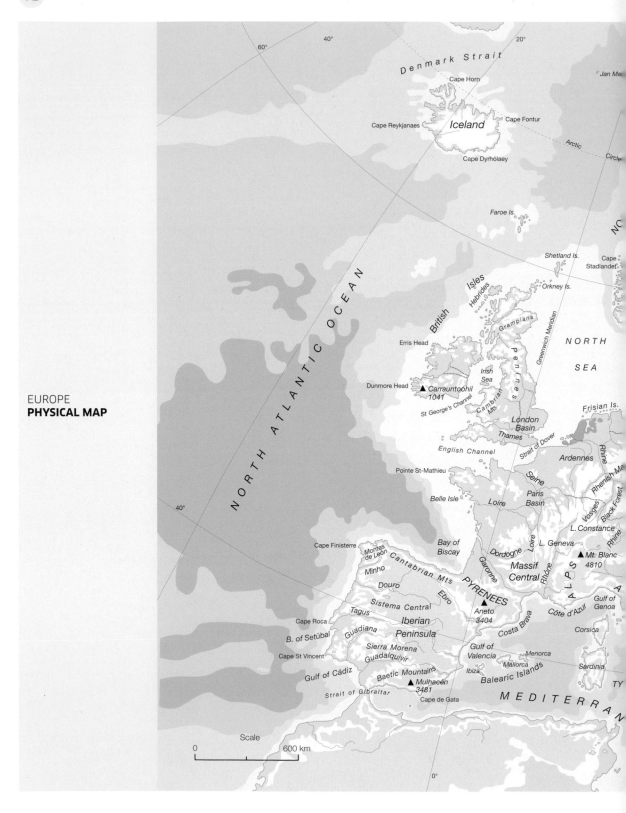

EUROPE
PHYSICAL MAP

Denmark Strait

Cape Horn

Jan Ma

Cape Reykjanaes

Iceland

Cape Fontur

Arctic

Circle

Cape Dyrhólaey

Faroe Is.

Shetland Is.

Cape Stadlandet

NC

British Isles

Hebrides

Orkney Is.

Grampians

Greenwich Meridian

NORTH SEA

Erris Head

Irish Sea

Pennines

Dunmore Head ▲ Carrauntoohil 1041

St George's Channel

Cambrian Mts

Frisian Is.

London Basin

Thames

Strait of Dover

Ardennes

Rhine

English Channel

Rhenish Ma

Pointe St-Mathieu

Seine

Paris Basin

Vosges

Black Forest

Belle Isle

Loire

L. Constance

Rhine

Bay of Biscay

Dordogne

Loire L. Geneva

▲ Mt. Blanc 4810

Cape Finisterre

Montes de León

Cantabrian Mts

Minho

Garonne

Massif Central

Rhône

A

Gulf of Genoa

Douro

Ebro

PYRENEES

ALPS

Côte d'Azur

Corsica

Sistema Central

▲ Aneto 3404

Tagus

Cape Roca

Iberian Peninsula

Costa Brava

B. of Setúbal

Guadiana

Gulf of Valencia

Menorca

Cape St Vincent

Sierra Morena

Guadalquivir

Mallorca

Ibiza

Sardinia

Balearic Islands

TY

Gulf of Cádiz

Baetic Mountains ▲ Mulhacén 3481

Strait of Gibraltar

Cape de Gata

MEDITERRAN

NORTH ATLANTIC OCEAN

40°

40°

60°

40°

20°

0°

Scale

0   600 km

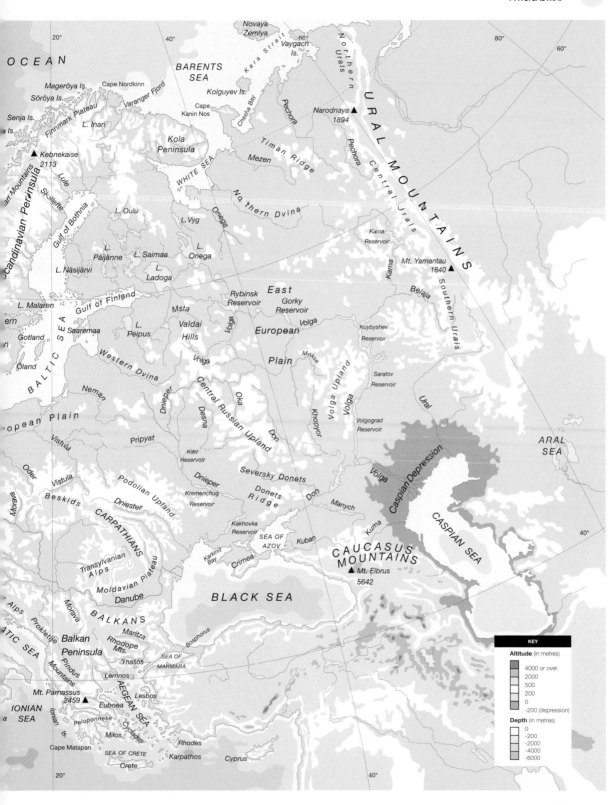

OCEAN

BARENTS
SEA

Novaya
Zemlya

Vaygach
Is.

Kara Strait

Kolguyev Is.

Northern Urals

URAL MOUNTAINS

Mageröya Is.
Cape Nordkinn
Söröya Is.
Varanger Fjord
Senja Is.
Is.
Finnmark Plateau
L. Inari

Cape
Kanin Nos

Chesha Bay

Pechora

Narodnaya
1894

Kebnekaise
2113

Kola
Peninsula

Mezen

Timan Ridge

Pechora

Central Urals

Scandinavian Peninsula

Lule
Skellefte

WHITE SEA

Northern Dvina

Kama
Reservoir

Kama

Mt. Yamantau
1640

L. Oulu

L. Vyg

Onega

L.
Päijänne
L. Saimaa
L.
Onega

L. Näsijärvi

L.
Ladoga

Gulf of Bothnia

Rybinsk
Reservoir

East

Gorky
Reservoir

Kuybyshev
Reservoir

Belaja

Southern Urals

L. Malaren

Gulf of Finland

Msta

European

Volga

Saratov
Reservoir

Gotland

Saaremaa

L.
Peipus

Valdai
Hills

Plain

Moksa

Volga Upland

Öland

BALTIC SEA

Western Dvina

Volga

Khopyor

Volga

Volgograd
Reservoir

ARAL
SEA

opean Plain

Neman

Dnieper

Desna

Central Russian Upland

Oka

Don

Ural

Vistula

Pripyat

Kiev
Reservoir

Volga

Caspian Depression

Oder

Vistula

Beskids

Podolian Upland

Dniester

Severksy Donets

Dnieper

Kremenchug
Reservoir

Donets
Ridge

Don

Manych

Kuma

CASPIAN SEA

Morava

CARPATHIANS

Kakhovka
Reservoir

SEA OF
AZOV

Kuban

Transylvanian
Alps

Moldavian Plateau

Danube

Karkinit
Bay

Crimea

CAUCASUS
MOUNTAINS

40°

Moravo

BALKANS

BLACK SEA

Mt. Elbrus
5642

Alps

Prokletije

Pindus Mountains

Balkan
Peninsula

Rhodope
Mts.

Maritza

Bosphorus

ATIC SEA

Thasos

SEA OF
MARMARA

Lemnos

AEGEAN SEA

Mt. Parnassus
2459

Lesbos

Euboea

IONIAN
a SEA

Peloponnese

Ionian Is.

Milos

Cyclades

Cape Matapan

SEA OF CRETE

Crete

Rhodes

Karpathos

Cyprus

KEY		
Altitude (in metres)		
4000 or over		
2000		
500		
200		
0		
-200 (depression)		
Depth (in metres)		
0		
-200		
-2000		
-4000		
-6000		

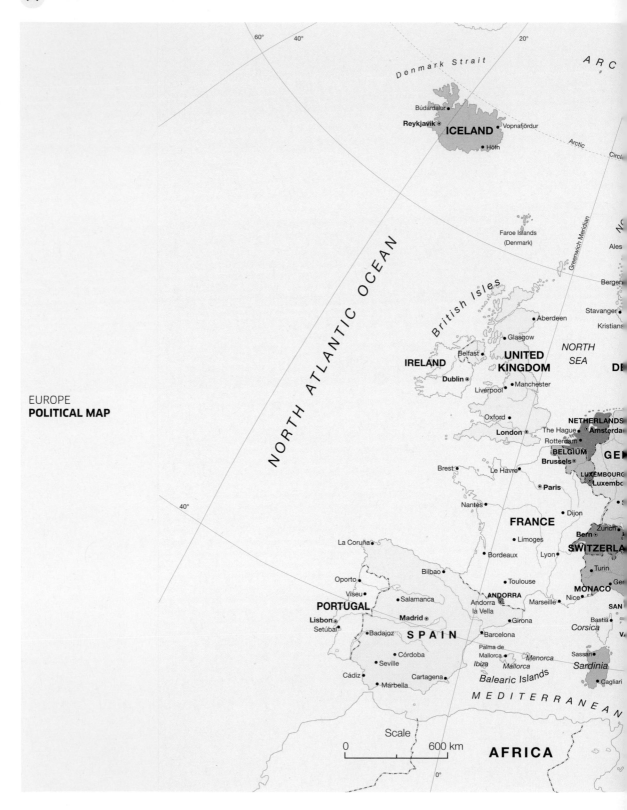

EUROPE
POLITICAL MAP

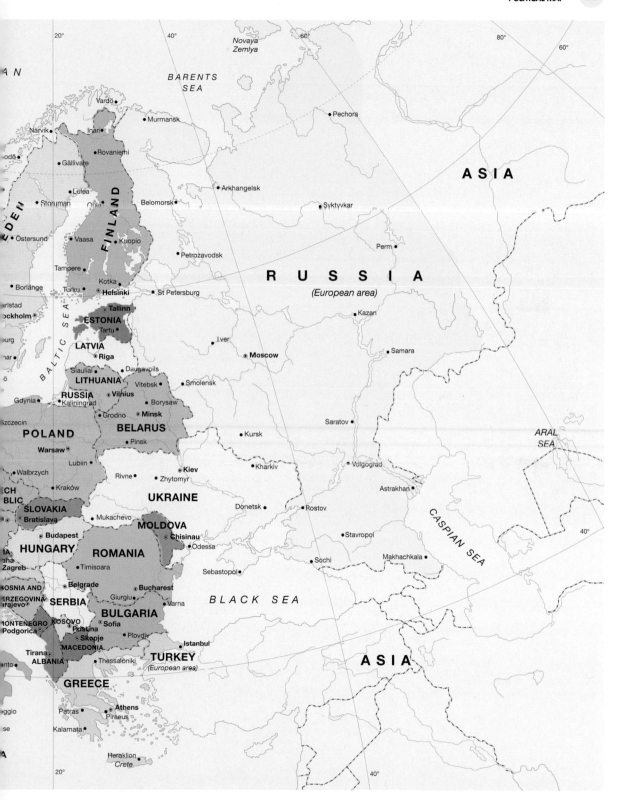

20°   40°   60°   80°   60°

*Novaya
Zemlya*

*BARENTS
SEA*

• Vardö

Narvik •   • Inari   • Pechora

odö •   • Murmansk

• Rovaniemi

• Gällivare   A S I A

• Luleå   • Arkhangelsk

Storuman •   Belomorsk •   • Syktyvkar

• Vaasa   • Kuopio   Perm •

Östersund •   F I N L A N D

Tampere •   R U S S I A

Borlänge •   Kotka •   *(European area)*
rlstad   Turku •   • St Petersburg
ckholm   • Helsinki   • Kazan

Tallinn   • Iver   • Samara
urg   ESTONIA
Tartu   • Moscow

LATVIA
har •   • Riga   • Daugavpils

Siauliai •   • Smolensk   A R A L
LITHUANIA   • Vitebsk   S E A
Gdynia •   • Vilnius
RUSSIA   • Borysaw   Saratov •
Kaliningrad •   • Minsk   • Volgograd
zczecin •   • Grodno
BELARUS   • Kursk   CASPIAN SEA
POLAND   • Pinsk
Warsaw ⊙   • Kharkiv   Astrakhan •
Walbrzych •   Lublin •   • Kiev
• Kraków   Rivne •   • Zhytomyr   40°
CH
BLIC   UKRAINE   • Donetsk   • Rostov
SLOVAKIA   • Mukachevo
⊙ Bratislava   MOLDOVA   • Stavropol
⊙ Budapest   • Chisinau   Makhachkala •
HUNGARY   ROMANIA   • Odessa   Sochi •
aha   • Timisoara
Zagreb   • Sebastopol
OSNIA AND   • Belgrade   • Bucharest
ERZEGOVINA   Giurgiu •   B L A C K   S E A
arajevo •   SERBIA   • Varna
ONTENEGRO   BULGARIA
Podgorica •   KOSOVO   • Sofia
Pristina •   • Plovdiv
Tirana •   Skopje •   • Istanbul
ALBANIA   MACEDONIA   TURKEY   A S I A
anto •   • Thessaloniki   *(European area)*
GREECE
ggio •   Patras •   • Athens
se   • Piraeus
Kalamata •

Heraklion
Crete

20°   40°

GEOGRAPHICAL WONDERS

Europe is the second-smallest continent in the world after Oceania. It is mostly very flat, with an average height of just 300 metres. However, the mountain ranges of Europe, such as the Pyrénées, the Alps and the Caucasus, reach as high as 5000 metres.

ATLANTIC HEIGHTS
SCANDINAVIA AND ICELAND

High peaks

The highest peaks in northern Europe are found in Scandinavia. Mount Galdhøppigen, in Norway, is the highest in the region at 2469 metres.

Alpine ranges
Typical Alpine landscapes have lakes surrounded by snow-capped peaks.

WESTERN EUROPE
ITALY – FRANCE

Mont Blanc

The most famous peak in Europe is Mont Blanc. Officially, it is 4810 metres high. However, the layer of snow at the summit can add between 10 and 15 metres, depending on the time of year. The peak lies on the border between France and Italy.

SPAIN
LA MANCHA

Spain's central plains

La Mancha is the largest plain on the Iberian Peninsula. The plain is split in two by the mountains of Toledo. The highest summits are Villuercas, at 1603 metres, and Rocigalgo, at 1448 metres. The area is famed for its traditional windmills.

RUSSIA
GLACIAL LAKES

The Valdai plateau

The Valdai plateau is located halfway between the Russian cities of St Petersburg and Moscow. The great plateau is drained by the rivers Volga and Dnieper, among others. Throughout the area, there are many beautiful glacial lakes.

CAUCASUS - RUSSIA
MOUNT ELBRUS

Highest peak

Mount Elbrus is the highest peak in Europe at 5642 metres high. The mountain is located on the northern edge of the Caucasus Mountains, near the Russian-Georgian border. Mount Elbrus is a volcano that has been dormant for more than 2000 years. Its summit is covered by a permanent layer of ice and more than 20 glaciers. The mountain is very popular among skiers and snowboarders.

Mount Elbrus
Located on the border
between Europe and Asia.

RUSSIA
RIVER SYSTEMS

Floodplains

The gently flowing rivers in western Russia deposit mud and rock as they pass by, to create areas called alluvial floodplains. The soil in the floodplains is rich in nutrients and is used to grow all kinds of crops, including cereals, potatoes and beets.

THE ALPS
IN PROFILE

Mountain chains, such as the Alps, are formed by folds and breaks in the Earth's crust. Erosion wears away at the mountains, and rivers carve valleys that separate one mountain from another. High plateaus, such as the Massif Central in France, are often found next to the rocky peaks.

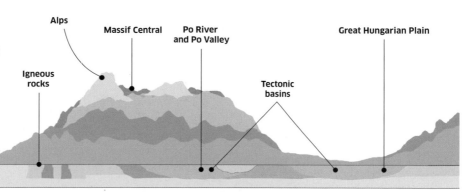

Alps

Massif Central

Po River and Po Valley

Great Hungarian Plain

Igneous rocks

Tectonic basins

Atlantic Ocean

THE ALPS

The Alps is the main mountain range of central Europe. These mountains stretch from Austria and Slovenia in the east, through Italy, Switzerland, Liechtenstein and Germany to France in the west. With their snow-capped peaks, the Alps have been shaped by thousands of years of glacial erosion.

Snow-capped The mighty Alpine peaks.

Vulture

The bearded vulture, which is in danger of extinction, has been reintroduced to the Alps.

GLACIERS
Each year, 3 per cent of Alpine glacier ice is lost as a result of global warming.

Mountain goat

This agile animal moves easily around the rocky terrain.

France
Mont Blanc is the highest mountain in the Alps. An 11-kilometre tunnel runs through the mountain.

Italy
This satellite view shows the Alps in Italy. The mountains cover an area of 300,000 square kilometres.

SIGHTS
DATA FILE

Facts about the Alps
The Alps is the longest mountain range in Europe. About 16 million people live in the Alpine region.

❶ **Length of mountain range:**
1200 kilometres

❷ **Ecosystems:**
Temperate deciduous forest, alpine pasture

❸ **Highest peak:**
Mont Blanc (4810 metres)

ITALY
DOLOMITES NATIONAL PARK

Typical vegetation
The landscape of the Dolomites National Park is dominated by coniferous forests. About 1400 different species of plant grow in the park.

ÖTZI
THE ICE MAN

The mummy and his weapons
In 1991, the mummified body of a man was found in the ice on the border between Italy and Austria. The body was more than 5000 years old and had been preserved by the ice. The man has been named Ötzi the Ice Man. Next to his body lay his weapons: an axe, a knife and a bow and arrows.

Studies suggest that Ötzi died during a fight.

Holidays

The slopes offer all kinds of activities, from mountaineering and hiking to snowboarding and skiing.

SNOW
SKIING SEASON

Lech–Zürs, Austria
One of Europe's most visited ski resorts, the area's steep slopes and snowy climate mean that its skiing season lasts from November to late April.

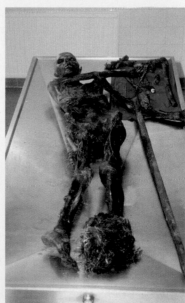

THE RIVER DANUBE

Nearly 2900 kilometres long, the Danube is the second-longest river in Europe. The river supports many different industries, including tourism, fishing and transport.

60
out of 300
The number of the Danube's tributaries that are navigable.

MAJOR CITIES ON THE RIVER

Course

The Danube rises in the town of Donaueschingen in Germany's Black Forest. It flows from there to the Black Sea. The river passes through 10 countries: Germany, Austria, Hungary, Slovakia, Croatia, Serbia, Bulgaria, Romania, Moldova and Ukraine.

POLLUTION
INDUSTRY

Chemicals

The River Danube flows through densely populated and industrialized areas, where there are nuclear power plants, factories and farms. Many chemicals leak into the river, and its waters are badly polluted.

Fishermen

Fishing is an important industry on the Danube. This Romanian fisherman is holding two sturgeon that he caught in the river.

Suspension bridge
A symbol of
Budapest,
in Hungary.

Budapest
This is a night scene of
the Hungarian capital
city, through which
the river flows.

Danube Delta
About 15,000 people
live in the Danube
Delta, which is
a UNESCO World
Heritage Site.

Capital cities
The Danube is the only river
in Europe to pass through four
capital cities: Vienna, Bratislava,
Budapest and Belgrade.

Under control
Dykes along the banks of the
river stop it from flooding.
There are also hydroelectric
power plants built across the
river to provide electricity.

Ships
The Danube is navigable
by large ocean ships from
the Black Sea to Brăila in
Romania, and by smaller
river ships to Kelheim,
Bavaria, in Germany.

CLIMATE

Most of Europe has a temperate climate, but in the north and south, the temperatures can be more extreme. Countries to the west have mild climates that are moderated by the Atlantic Ocean. In the south, the Alps prevent cold winds from affecting the Mediterranean coast, where it can be very hot in summer.

Ice floes in Norway
Ice floats in the sea off the coast of Spitsbergen Island, Norway. Temperatures there remain below 0 °C for most of the year.

STRONG WINDS
CANARY ISLANDS, SPAIN

The Sirocco

In the summer, a strong wind from North Africa blows across southern Europe. Called the Sirocco, it is a hot and dry wind that blows off the Sahara Desert. It sometimes carries thick clouds of sand, which can cause health problems such as stinging eyes.

RAIN
LONDON, UNITED KINGDOM

Moderate climate

The climate in London is moderate. During the summer, the average maximum temperature ranges between 21 °C and 24 °C. In the summer months, the city's many parks are full of people. Londoners make the most of the open spaces to exercise and picnic. The winter months are much colder, with temperatures dropping to 2 °C or lower. It can rain throughout the year in London but rainfall is usually higher in the colder winter months. The annual average rainfall is about 600 millimetres.

Paris, France
In recent years, the temperatures in European cities have been higher than usual.

20,000
The number of people who died during the European heatwave of 2003.

Heatwave
Between 3 and 13 August 2003, the average temperature in Paris, France, was 40 °C.

HEATWAVE
CRISIS IN EUROPE

Consequences
In 2003, there was a heatwave throughout Europe. Southern countries, such as Spain, Italy and Portugal, had the highest temperatures. Alicante in Spain saw temperatures reach 47 °C.

France
During the heatwave, temperatures in France reached their highest since 1950. In Paris, the temperature reached 40 °C during the day. The warmest night was on 11–12 August, when the temperature only dropped to 25.5 °C.

Mediterranean
The climate of Porto Venere, Italy (left), is extreme. The summers are often incredibly hot and the winters are very cold.

Greece
In winter on the Greek islands, it rains one day in three. However, the sea remains as warm as 15 °C even in the middle of winter.

THE DECIDUOUS FOREST HABITAT

Much of continental Europe is covered in temperate forests.
These forests are home to deciduous trees such as oak,
beech and lime. Many animals, small and large, live in the
forests, including squirrels, rabbits, wild boar, deer, foxes,
eagles, owls and other birds of prey.

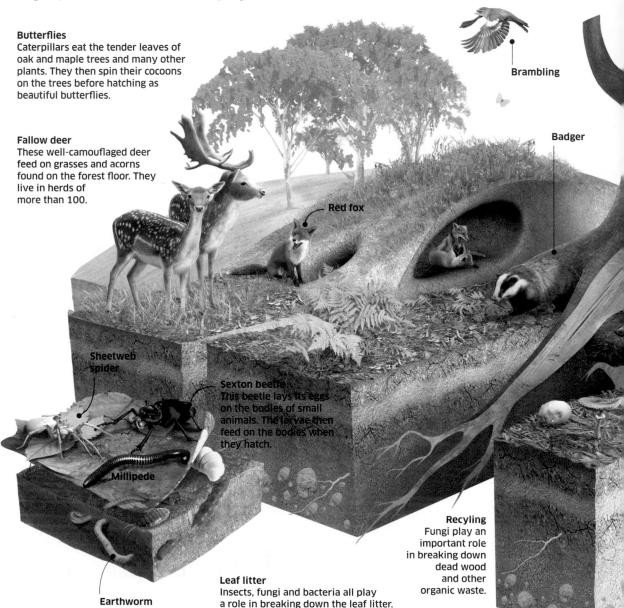

European green woodpecker

Brambling

Badger

Butterflies
Caterpillars eat the tender leaves of
oak and maple trees and many other
plants. They then spin their cocoons
on the trees before hatching as
beautiful butterflies.

Fallow deer
These well-camouflaged deer
feed on grasses and acorns
found on the forest floor. They
live in herds of
more than 100.

Red fox

**Sheetweb
spider**

Sexton beetle
This beetle lays its eggs
on the bodies of small
animals. The larvae then
feed on the bodies when
they hatch.

Millipede

Recyling
Fungi play an
important role
in breaking down
dead wood
and other
organic waste.

Earthworm

Leaf litter
Insects, fungi and bacteria all play
a role in breaking down the leaf litter.
This important process provides
the trees and other foliage with
essential nutrients.

Grey squirrel

Common pipistrelle

Eagle owl
This solitary animal rests during the day and hunts at night. The eagle owl has been known to hunt other birds, including other owls. Its deep cry can be heard up to 3 kilometres away.

Wild boar
The wild boar can reach a maximum weight of 100 kilograms. It has an excellent sense of smell that it uses to detect food and the presence of predators.

Pine marten

Common hedgehog

Common pheasant

Rabbit

Edible dormouse

Building tunnels
Rabbits dig complex tunnel systems, called warrens, in the forest floor. Each warren has many entrances and exits.

LIFE IN THE WOOD

Hibernation
Many mammals, such as bats (below), sleep during the coldest weeks of winter. This is called hibernation. During hibernation, their body temperature and breathing are lower than normal. They use the fat reserves stored in their bodies during the warmer months to survive the winter.

AUTUMN DECIDUOUS TREES

Falling leaves
During the autumn months, the deciduous trees of Europe's forests lose their leaves. The autumn starts in September. New leaves begin to grow in the spring, which starts in March.

Turning brown
Plants need sunlight to produce the chlorophyll that keeps their leaves green. With less light in autumn, the trees stop producing chlorophyll and the leaves turn red, brown and yellow.

POPULATION

In the 1900s, about 25 per cent of the world's population lived in Europe. Today, the populations of other continents have grown to overtake Europe, but it is still a densely populated continent. It is mostly very developed, with modern cities and a high standard of living.

City of London
The City is London's financial district. It is lively and full of activity during the day, but much quieter at night.

LONDON, UNITED KINGDOM
A POPULOUS CITY

Business centre
London, the capital of the United Kingdom, is home to about 7.83 million people. Built along the banks of the River Thames, it is a cosmopolitan city and world financial centre.

Tower Bridge
This striking bridge opened in 1894. The bridge allows vehicles and pedestrians to cross from one side of the River Thames to the other. It also has an electrohydraulic system that enables it to open to let ships and large vessels travel down the Thames.

Traditions
The UK has managed to balance modern living with the traditions of the past. As a result, the country has a rich and varied cultural heritage.

BELGIUM
BRUSSELS

Home of the European Union

Brussels is one of the most densely populated cities in Europe. The city is the capital of Belgium and also the administrative headquarters of the European Union (EU). Most of the city's inhabitants speak French, while some speak Flemish. The Royal Palace (below) was built in 1779 and is the official residence of the king of Belgium.

BULGARIA
JOINING THE EUROPEAN UNION

Between east and west

For many centuries, Bulgaria was ruled by the Ottoman Empire. After World War II, it was close to the Soviet Union. In January 2007, Bulgaria became a member of the European Union. The country's main ethnic groups are Bulgarians, Turks and Roma. The photo below shows Nesebar, an old resort town on the Black Sea, and a peasant in traditional Bulgarian clothes.

Naples
A street in the historic centre of the city.

ITALY
NAPLES

Picturesque but troubled

Naples, with about 1 million inhabitants, is the third largest city in Italy. The city has beautiful historic buildings, but it is plagued by a high rate of unemployment and has a high crime rate.

Street sales
A street seller offers rabbits for sale in Naples.

RUSSIAN FEDERATION
MOSCOW

Biggest city

Moscow has over 11.5 million inhabitants, making it the largest city in Europe. Built along the banks of the River Moskva, it is the capital of the Russian Federation. The city contains many fine historical buildings, including the Kremlin (below), a huge fortified palace at the centre of the city, which now serves as the official residency of the Russian president.

ECONOMY

Europe's economy is one of the strongest in the world. However, not all the countries in Europe share the same level of development – countries in the west tend to be more developed than those in the east. Trade, transport, finance, tourism and heavy industry drive the European economy.

Engadine Valley, Switzerland
The Engadine Valley sits at 1800 metres above sea level. It is surrounded by striking mountains, where skiing is a very popular pastime.

ALPS
TOURISM

Snow sports

Each year, snow sports attract millions of tourists to the Alps. These visitors provide the Alpine countries with a great economic boost.

Skiing
Skiers flock to the Alps.

TRANSPORT NETWORK
RAILWAYS

High-speed trains

Despite its many natural borders, the European transport network is highly developed. Due to the growth of trade with the East, the number of passengers and the volume of cargo coming into, and going out of, Europe has greatly increased. To solve the problem of congestion at airports and on motorways, the continent has a network of high-speed trains that connects many of Europe's main cities in just a few hours. For example, it is possible to travel from London to Paris in about two hours.

The Eurostar
These trains travel between London, Paris and Brussels.

CROPS
PRIMARY SECTOR

Bulgaria's roses

Roses have been grown in Bulgaria's Rose Valley for centuries. The region is the leading producer of rose oil, which is used in perfumes. Collecting the roses is done by hand, usually by women.

Bergheim, Germany
These blast furnaces are used in the production of steel.

FUEL
NATURAL GAS

The energy problem

Most European countries have to import gas. Around 60 per cent of Europe's gas is imported. Most comes from Russia. To avoid having to depend on Russia, many Western European countries are looking to use other energy sources, such as solar, wind and nuclear power.

A BLOCK OF NATIONS
UNITY IN EUROPE

The European Union

Most of the countries in Europe belong to the European Union (EU). Citizens of EU countries can travel and work anywhere within the EU. Most of the countries use the euro as currency. As of 2012, the countries in the EU are: Austria, Belgium, Bulgaria, Cyprus, Czech Republic, Denmark, Estonia, Finland, France, Germany, Greece, Hungary, Ireland, Italy, Latvia, Lithuania, Luxembourg, Malta, Netherlands, Poland, Portugal, Romania, Slovakia, Slovenia, Spain, Sweden and the United Kingdom.

Car factory
Germany, France and Italy are the main car manufacturers in Europe.

LOW COUNTRIES
POLDERS

Reclaiming land

Polders are low-lying pieces of land that are enclosed by barriers, called dykes, which separate the land from the sea. Water is pumped out of the low-lying land, which dries up to be used for farming. This technique was first used in the Netherlands in the 11th century.

LANGUAGES AND PEOPLE

There are three main language groups in Europe: 300 million people speak Slavic languages, such as Russian and Polish, 200 million speak Romance languages, such as French, Italian and Spanish; and another 200 million people speak Germanic languages, such as English, Swedish and German.

Protected

Finnish, Hungarian and Estonian are Uralic languages that are protected as national tongues. Other Uralic languages have been displaced by Russian.

Basque
Basque, spoken in parts of Spain and France, is the only European language that does not belong to the Indo-European group of languages.

Most spoken

Due to European colonialism between the 16th and 20th centuries, English, Spanish, French and Portuguese are among the most commonly spoken languages in the world.

Language
Speech is the most versatile form of communication.

Traditional dress

There were 16 million Muslims living in the EU in 2007, and most are immigrants or the children of immigrants. Many Muslim women cover their heads with a traditional veil.

Immigrants

Immigrants in Europe face many kinds of discrimination. Here, demonstrators in London campaign against the deportation of Nigerian immigrants.

NATIVE LANGUAGES OF EUROPE

Indo-European languages

Almost all European languages are descended from Indo-European languages. These were spoken by Asiatic tribes that invaded Europe 6000 years ago. They gave rise to a number of language families:

1. Albanian
2. Baltic
3. Celtic
4. Slavic
5. Germanic
6. Greek
7. Romance
8. Uralic

Romance languages

Descended from Latin, which was spread by the Roman Empire:

1. Spanish, or Castilian
2. Catalan
3. French
4. Portuguese
5. Italian
6. Romansh
7. Romanian

Religion

The largest religious groups in Europe are Christian churches:

1. **The Catholic Church**
   Based around the absolute authority of the Pope.

2. **Protestant Churches**
   Anglicans, Calvinists, Lutherans and others.

3. **Greek and Russian Orthodox Churches**
   Eastern European churches that do not recognize the authority of the Pope.

CASE STUDIES EUROPEAN IDENTITIES

AUSTRIA
AUSTRO-BAVARIAN

German dialect

The Austro-Bavarian dialect is spoken in Austria and in the southern German state of Bavaria. This dialect is the native tongue of about 12 million people.

SCANDINAVIA
SAMI

Fight for their rights

The last aboriginal European culture still survives in remote parts of northern Scandinavia and Russia. The Sami – also known as Lapps – number about 80,000 people.

THE BALKANS
GREECE

Cradle of civilization

Ancient Greece was one of the great civilizations of history. Today, modern Greeks consider themselves to be Western Europeans, although the country is located in the east of the continent.

ACROSS EUROPE
ROMA

Indian peoples

Also known as gypsies, the nomadic Roma people arrived in Europe from India in the 11th century. They number about 12 million people.

THE SAMI PEOPLE

The Sami, or Lapps, people are among the oldest inhabitants of
Europe. Scattered throughout the Scandinavian countries, they total
some 80,000 people. The Sami's traditional lifestyle changed first
with the arrival of Christianity in the region 1000 years ago,
then again with the technological advances of the 20th century.

FROM AFRICA TO EURASIA

A common heritage

The first modern humans left Africa
about 80,000 years ago and settled
in Oceania and Asia. A second
migration took place 35,000 years
ago to the Middle East, and the
Balkans. It is thought that 80 per
cent of Europeans have ancestors
who migrated at this time. It is
thought that the other 20 per cent
of Europeans came from the Middle
East about 10,000 years ago.

ADAPTATION TO THE CLIMATE

Fair skin

It is thought that as people moved
north from Africa to Europe, they
had less exposure to the Sun. As
a result, over time, their skin
became lighter.

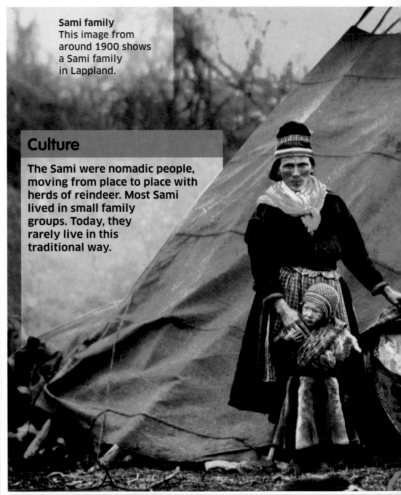

Sami family
This image from
around 1900 shows
a Sami family
in Lappland.

Culture

The Sami were nomadic people,
moving from place to place with
herds of reindeer. Most Sami
lived in small family
groups. Today, they
rarely live in this
traditional way.

Beliefs

The Sami religion focussed
on the worship of animal
and ancestral spirits. Today,
many are Christians and
follow Lutheranism.

Tools
The Sami are skilled craftspeople who carve tools and other implements from bone, wood, antlers and silver. Their carvings are often decorated with geometric patterns.

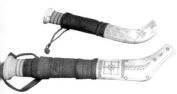

Identity
Although the Sami are spread across four countries (Norway, Sweden, Finland and Russia), they have their own flag (left).

Tents
The tents used by the Sami were similar to North American tepees. They were made from reindeer skins and were easy to take down as the tribe moved from place to place. Today, most of the Sami live in European-style houses.

Economy
Traditionally, the Sami were hunter-gatherers. Today, they are reindeer herders, and they are thought to have about half a million reindeer.

Shaman's drum
The Sami believed that the shaman was a link between them and the spirit world. During ceremonies, the shaman played a drum.

PRAGUE

Located in the heart of Europe, the Czech capital Prague has a rich musical tradition and was home to the famous composer Antonín Dvořák. The city has many tourist attractions, including museums, galleries, churches, synagogues, palaces and gardens.

Country	Czech Republic
Area	496 sq km
Population	1,258,106
Density	2537 people/sq km

SYMBOLS OF THE CITY

Astronomical clock

Prague's astronomical clock dates from the 15th century. It is one of the city's best-loved tourist attractions, and hundreds of visitors flock to stand under it each hour, waiting to see it working.

Charles Bridge

This famous bridge unites the old and new cities. It opened in 1503 and is 516 metres long and 9.5 metres wide. There are religious statues along it and those who stand on the bridge get a great view of Prague.

Population

According to 2006 data, 8.77 per cent of the population of Prague was foreign-born.

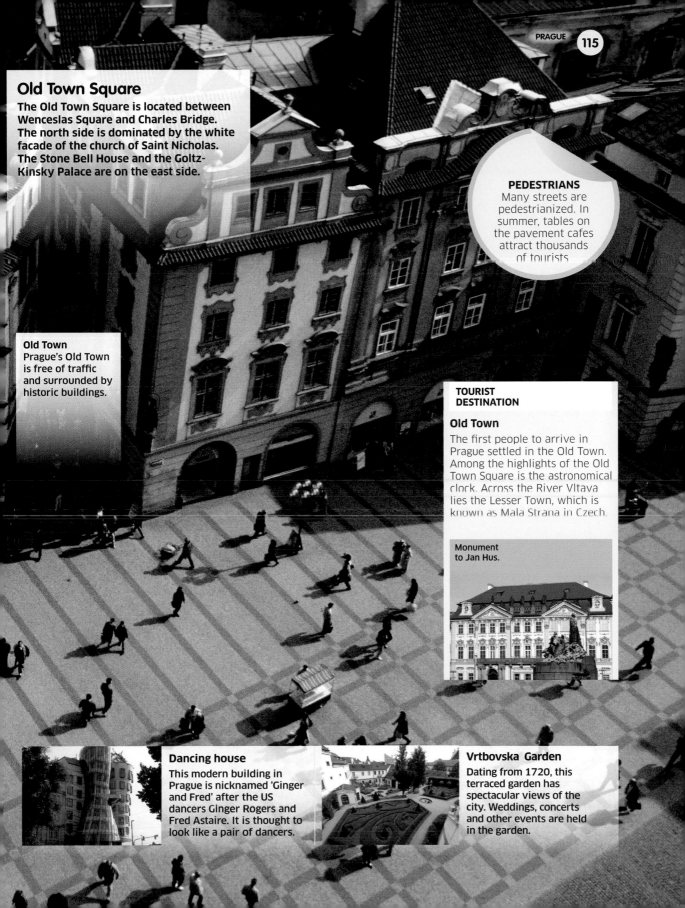

Old Town Square

The Old Town Square is located between Wenceslas Square and Charles Bridge. The north side is dominated by the white facade of the church of Saint Nicholas. The Stone Bell House and the Goltz-Kinsky Palace are on the east side.

PEDESTRIANS
Many streets are pedestrianized. In summer, tables on the pavement cafes attract thousands of tourists.

Old Town
Prague's Old Town is free of traffic and surrounded by historic buildings.

TOURIST DESTINATION

Old Town

The first people to arrive in Prague settled in the Old Town. Among the highlights of the Old Town Square is the astronomical clock. Across the River Vltava lies the Lesser Town, which is known as Mala Strana in Czech.

Monument to Jan Hus.

Dancing house

This modern building in Prague is nicknamed 'Ginger and Fred' after the US dancers Ginger Rogers and Fred Astaire. It is thought to look like a pair of dancers.

Vrtbovska Garden

Dating from 1720, this terraced garden has spectacular views of the city. Weddings, concerts and other events are held in the garden.

THE COLOSSEUM

In the 1ˢᵗ century AD, the Colosseum was built in Rome
by Emperor Vespasian. This amphitheatre seated up to
50,000 spectators. Today, the ruins of the Colosseum
are one of Rome's biggest tourist attractions.

THE COLOSSEUM
FACT FILE

Location:
Rome, Italy

Type:
Amphitheatre

Date opened:
AD 80

Capacity:
50,000

Dimensions:

48 m   188 m   156 m   524 m

Colossus

It is thought that the Colosseum
was named after the colossal
statue of Emperor Nero.

CORINTHIAN
COLUMN

IONIC
COLUMN

DIFFERENT
COLUMNS

Styles

The building had three
different types of column,
which were used to decorate
the outside walls: Doric, Ionic
and Corinthian.

Doric   Ionic   Corinthian

COLOSSEUM **UP CLOSE**

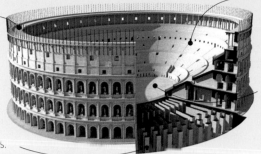

Sliding roof
A canvas roof protected the public from rain and sun.

Terraces
Seating was arranged according to social class. The better seats were made from marble, while the top section was made of wood.

Underground
Cells and cages were built underground for the gladiators and wild animals.

Arena
The Colosseum was used for bloody contests including mock sea battles, animal hunts, executions and dramas based on mythology.

1 MILLION
The number of tonnes of stone and brick that were used to construct the arches.

Walls
The walls were raised with blocks of stone, brick and limestone.

Ruins
After a series of earthquakes, much of the building has collapsed.

DORIC COLUMN

Colosseum
The outside view of the amphitheatre.

THE ALHAMBRA

This walled city in southern Spain is a beautiful complex of palaces, forts and gardens. It was home to the court of the Arab (Moorish) kingdom of Granada between the 13th and 15th centuries. The Alhambra is considered one of the greatest examples of Islamic art in Europe.

THE ALHAMBRA
FACT FILE

Date:
9th to 14th centuries

Location:
Granada, Spain

Structure:
Originally built for military purposes, the city was both a strong fortress and a palace. The Spanish added other buildings, such as the palace of Charles V.

JOINING THE SQUARES

Patio of the Lions
The garden displays the Muslim idea of Paradise. In each room, there are four waterfalls supported by 12 lions. The columns are joined with lace panels that let in sunlight.

Lion fountain
Made from marble, this is found in the central courtyard.

10,000
The number of inscriptions that adorn the Alhambra.

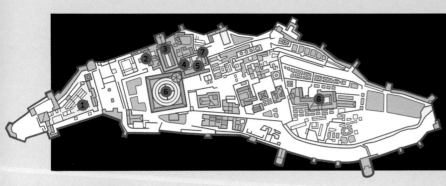

Architectural plan

1. Alcazaba
2. The Golden Room
3. Comares Palace
4. Palace of the Lions
5. Patio of the Lions
6. Palace of Charles V
7. Hall of the Kings
8. Monastery of St Francis

Last king

Boabdil was the last king of Moorish Spain. He was overthrown in 1492 by Catholic forces from the north.

Motto

On many of the walls, the inscriptions read: 'There is no god but Allah.'

The Alhambra
View of the building in Granada, southern Spain.

Court of the Myrtles

When the Alhambra was built, water was in short supply, so the large pond here was a symbol of wealth and power. The court is also called the Court of the Pond.

Palace of Charles V

The palace was built in the 16th century. It is a Renaissance-style double-storey building with a large, circular courtyard. Today, it houses the Museum of Fine Arts.

ASIA
INTRODUCTION

Asia makes up one-third of the Earth's continental land mass. The centre of the continent is dominated by a large plateau and huge mountain ranges. Great rivers flow across Asia, including the Yangtze in China and the Ganges in India. The Earth's lowest place, the Dead Sea, can be found on the border of Israel and Jordan. The continent also has a great range of peoples. There are many different ethnic groups in Asia, from the Sherpas of the Himalayas to the Roma. Each of them have their own beliefs, language and lifestyle.

JORDAN
THE SANDSTONE IN THE REGION NEAR THE ANCIENT CITY OF PETRA IS CARVED INTO UNIQUE ROCK FORMATIONS, SUCH AS THESE CANYONS.

ASIA
PHYSICAL MAP

NORTH
AMERICA

NORTH
AMERICA

NORTH ATLANTIC OCEAN

Greenwich Meridian

Arctic Circle

ARCTIC OCEAN

North Pole

BARENTS
SEA

NORWEGIAN SEA

NORTH SEA

BALTIC SEA

Svalbard

Franz Josef
Land

Novaya
Zemlya

KARA SEA

Severnaya
Zemlya

October
Revolution
Is.

Komsomolets Is.

Bolshevik Is.

C. Zhelaniya

Bely Is.

Yamal
Peninsula

Gydan
Peninsula

Gt Lyakhovsky Is.

Kotelny Is.

New
Siberian
Islands

Novaya Sibir

Medvezhyi
Is.

Wrangel
Is.

EAST SIBERIAN
SEA

LAPTEV SEA

Byrranga Mts.

Taymyr
Peninsula

L. Taymyr

Begichev Is.

Cape Dezhnev

Bering Strait

Chukchi
Peninsula

Anadyr-
Plateau

Anadyr

Koryma

Indigirka

Pobeda
▲ 3147

KOLYMA MTS.

CHERSKY RANGE

Yana

VERKHOYANSK RANGE

Lena

Aldan

Kotuy

Lower Tunguska

Central
Siberian
Plateau

Yenisey

West Siberian
Plain

Ob

L. Zaysan

ALTAI MTS.

SAYAN MTS.

Mt. Belukha
▲ 4506

L. Baikal

YABLONOVYY MTS.

GOBI DESERT

Mt. Chajchan Ubi
▲ 4362

GT. KHINGAN RANGE

MANCHURIA

Amur

SIKHOTE-ALIN

Bohai

KOREA

SEA OF
JAPAN

Hokkaido

Honshu

▲ Mt. Fuji
3776

Sumisu

Tori Shima

Iô-Jima

Sakata

Kunashir

Iturup

Kuril Islands

Lopatka

Kamchatka
Peninsula

Kyuzhnevskaya Sopka
▲ 4750

SREDINNY RANGE

Komandorski Is.

Karaginsky Is.

BERING
SEA

Aleutian Is.

SEA OF OKHOTSK

Shelikhov
Gulf

C. Elizabeth

Sakhalin

Tartar Strait

Shantar

Dzhugdzhur Mts.

SIBERIA

Syr Darya

Amu Darya

Ural

ARAL
SEA

L. Balkhash

Lenin Peak
▲ 7134

URAL MOUNTAINS

Mt. Narodnaya
▲ 1894

Mt. Yamantau
▲ 1640

Volga

Caspian Depression

CASPIAN SEA

Sea of
Azov

BLACK SEA

CAUCASUS

Mt. Elbrus
5642 ▲

PONTIC MTS.

Mt. Ararat
5165 ▲

Mt. Damavand
5605 ▲

ZAGROS MTS.

ELBURZ MTS.

Euphrates

SYRIAN
DESERT

EUROPE

Anatolia

TAURUS MTS.

Sea of
Marmara

Bosporus

AEGEAN SEA

Cyprus

MEDITERRANEAN SEA

Sinai
Peninsula

Suez Canal

50°

60°

70°

80°

160°

140°

160°

140°

120°

100°

90°

80°

60°

40°

20°

80°

60°

40°

20°

70°

60°

50°

40°

30°

30°

40°

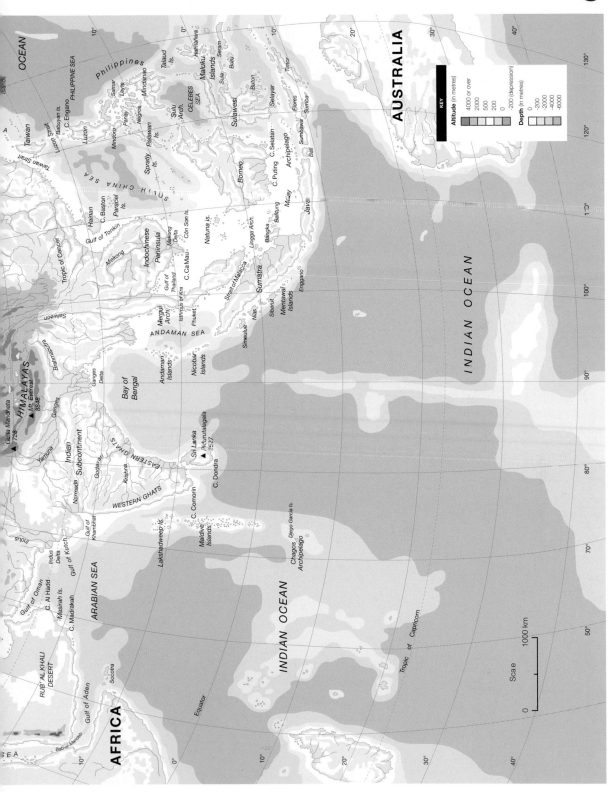

OCEAN

Philippines

PHILIPPINE SEA

Islands

C. Engano

C. Luzon · Babuyan Is.

Luzon Strait

Taiwan

Taiwan Strait

Mindoro

Panay

Negros

Samar

Leyte

Talaud
Is.

Mindanao

CELEBES
SEA

Sulu
Arch.

Palawan

Spratly
Is.

SOUTH CHINA SEA

Maluku
Islands

Halmahera

Buru

Seram

Sula

Buton

Selayar

Sulawesi

C. Selatan

C. Puting

Borneo

Archipelago

Flores

Sumbawa

Sumba

Timor

Bali

Java

Belitung

Bangka

Lingga Arch.

Natuna Is.

Mekong
Delta

Côn Son Is.

C. Ca Mau

Paracel
Is.

C. Baston

Hainan

Gulf of Tonkin

Gulf of
Thailand

Mekong

Indochinese
Peninsula

Tropic of Cancer

Salween

Brahmaputra

HIMALAYAS

Gauri Mandhata
▲ 7728

▲ Mt. Everest
8848

Ganges

Yamuna

Ganges
Delta

Indian
Subcontinent

Godavari

Krishna

EASTERN GHATS

Sri Lanka

▲Pidurutalagala
2527

C. Dondra

Strait of Malacca

Isthmus of Kra

Phuket

Mergui
Arch.

ANDAMAN SEA

Andaman
Islands

Nicobar
Islands

Simeulue

Nias

Siberut

Mentawai
Islands

Enggano

Sumatra

Bay of
Bengal

WESTERN GHATS

C. Comorin

Maldive
Islands

Lakshadweep Is.

Chagos
Archipelago

Diego Garcia Is.

Narmada

Indus
Delta

Indus

Gulf of
Khambhat

Gulf of Kutch

Gulf of Oman

C. Al Hadd

Masirah Is.

C. Madrakah

ARABIAN SEA

RUB' AL KHALI
DESERT

Gulf of Aden

Socotra

Bab-el-Mandeb

AFRICA

Equator

INDIAN OCEAN

Tropic of Capricorn

INDIAN OCEAN

AUSTRALIA

Scale

1000 km

KEY

Altitude (in metres)

4000 or over
2000
500
200
0
-200 (depression)

Depth (in metres)

0
-200
-2000
-4000
-6000

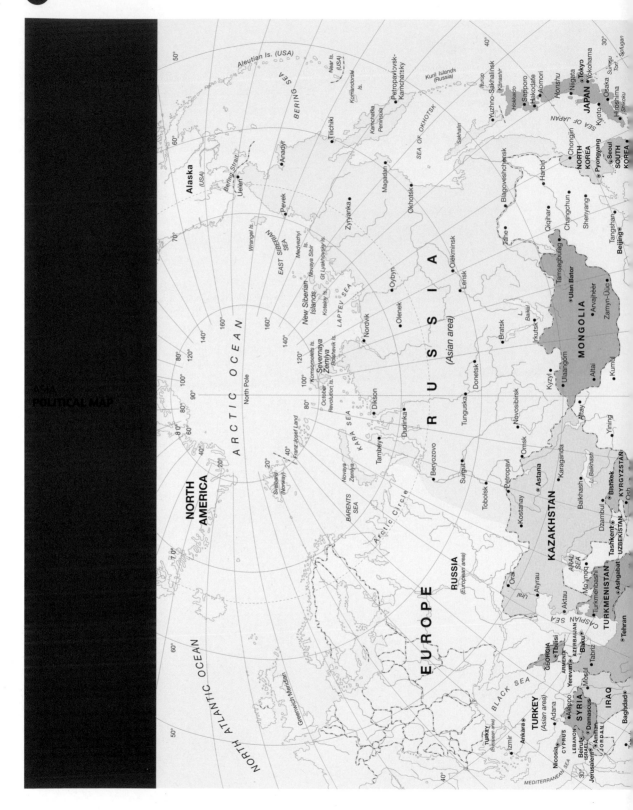

ASIA
POLITICAL MAP

50°

Aleutian Is. (USA)

Near Is. (USA)

Kuril Islands (Russia)

Iturup

40°   30°

Shiretoko
Tori

BERING SEA

Komandorski Is.

Petropavlovsk-Kamchatsky

Yuzhno-Sakhalinsk

Kunashir

Sapporo

Niigata

Yokohama

JAPAN Tokyo

Osaka

Kyoto

Shikoku

Hokkaido

Honshu

Hakodate

Aomori

Hiroshima

60°

Kamchatka Peninsula

Sakhalin

SEA OF JAPAN

SEA OF OKHOTSK

Chongjin

NORTH KOREA

Pyongyang

Seoul

SOUTH KOREA

Alaska (USA)

Bering Strait

Uelen

Tilichiki

Anadyr

Magadan

Okhotsk

Blagoveshchensk

Harbin

Qiqihar

Changchun

Shenyang

Tangshan

Beijing

70°

Pevek

Zyryanka

Yakhe

Tamsagbulag

Ulan Bator

Arvaiheer

Zamyn-Üüd

MONGOLIA

Wrangel Is.

EAST SIBERIAN SEA

Medvezhyi Is.

Novaya Sibir

Gt Lyakhovsky Is.

Oymyakon

Olëkminsk

Lensk

L. Baikal

Bratsk

Irkutsk

Ulaangom

Altai

Yining

Kumul

160°

140°

120°

New Siberian Islands

Koteiny Is.

LAPTEV SEA

Nordvik

Olenëk

R U S S I A

(Asian area)

Kyzyl

Altay

ARCTIC   OCEAN

80°

100°

90°

North Pole

Komsomolets Is.

Severnaya Zemlya

October Revolution Is.

Bolshevik Is.

Dikson

Donetsk

Novosibirsk

Tunguska

Karaganda

80°

60°

80°

Franz-Josef Land

KARA SEA

Dudinka

Beryozovo

Surgut

Omsk

L. Balkhash

Balkhash

Bishkek

KYRGYZSTAN

Osh

NORTH AMERICA

40°

20°

Novaya Zemlya

Tambey

Petropavl

Astana

KAZAKHSTAN

Dzhambul

Tashkent

UZBEKISTAN

Svalbard (Norway)

BARENTS SEA

Tobolsk

Kostanay

Aralsk

ARAL SEA

Ashgabat

TURKMENISTAN

Tehran

Arctic Circle

EUROPE

RUSSIA (European area)

Oral

Atyrau

Aktau

CASPIAN SEA

Moynoq

Turkmenbashi

70°

Ural

AZERBAIJAN

Baku

GEORGIA

Tbilisi

ARMENIA

Yerevan

Tabriz

60°

Greenwich Meridian

BLACK SEA

TURKEY (Asian area)

Ankara

Mosul

IRAQ

Baghdad

NORTH ATLANTIC OCEAN

50°

40°

Izmir

TURKEY (European area)

Adana

Aleppo

SYRIA

Damascus

LEBANON

Beirut

ISRAEL

Jerusalem

Amman

JORDAN

Nicosia

CYPRUS

30°

MEDITERRANEAN SEA

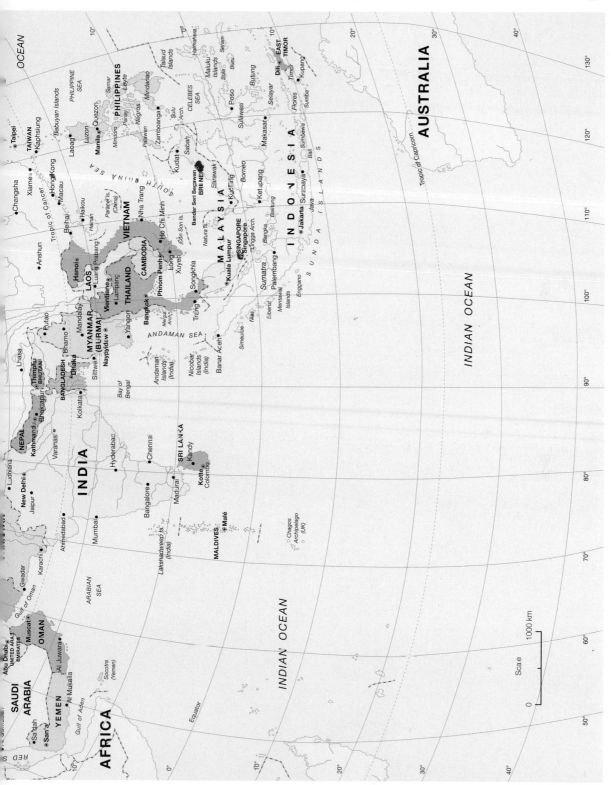

OCEAN

10°

ASIA

PHILIPPINE
SEA

PHILIPPINES

Talaud
Islands

Halmahera

EAST
TIMOR

130°

AUSTRALIA

Taipei
TAIWAN
Kaohsiung
Babuyan Islands

Luzon
Samar
Panay Leyte

Mindanao

Maluku
Islands

Sula

Seram

Buru

Dili
Timor

Kupang

120°

Changsha
Xiamen
Hongkong
Macau

Quezon
Manila
Mindoro
Negros

CELEBES
SEA

Zamboanga
Sulu
Arch.

Poso

Sulawesi

Makasar
Selayar

Butung

Flores

Sumba

Sumbawa

Bali

Tropic of Capricorn

30°

Tropic of Cancer
Beihai
Haikou
Hainan

Paracel Is.
(China)

SOUTH
CHINA
SEA

Nha Trang

Palawan
Sabah
Kudat

Bandar Seri Begawan
BRUNEI
Sarawak
Kuching

Borneo

Ketapang

110°

Anshun

VIETNAM

Ho Chi Minh

Côn Son Is.

Natuna Is.

INDONESIA

Belitung

Bangka

100°

INDIAN OCEAN

Hanoi
LAOS
Luang Prabang
Vientiane
Lampang

THAILAND

CAMBODIA
Phnom Penh
Long
Xuyen
Bangkok
Songkhla
Trang

MALAYSIA
Kuala Lumpur
SINGAPORE
Singapore
Lingga Arch.

Sumatra
Palembang

Jakarta
Surabaya
Java

SUNDA ISLANDS

90°

Putao
Bhamo
Mandalay

MYANMAR
(BURMA)
Naypyidaw
Yangon

ANDAMAN SEA

Mergui
Arch.

Banar Aceh

Siberut
Mentawai
Islands

Nias

Enggano

Lhasa
Thimphu
BHUTAN
BANGLADESH
Dhaka
Sittwe

Andaman
Islands
(India)

Nicobar
Islands
(India)

Simeulue

Bay of
Bengal

NEPAL
Kathmandu
Bhaktapur
Kolkata

Varanasi

Hyderabad

Chennai

SRI LANKA
Kandy

Kotte
Colombo

80°

Ludhiana
New Delhi
Jaipur

INDIA

Bangalore
Madurai

Ahmedabad

Mumbai

MALDIVES
Malé

Lakshadweep Is.
(India)

Chagos
Archipelago
(UK)

70°

Gwadar
Gulf of Oman
Karachi

ARABIAN
SEA

INDIAN OCEAN

60°

1000 km

Abu Dhabi
UNITED ARAB
EMIRATES
Muscat
OMAN
Al Juwara

Scale

SAUDI
ARABIA

YEMEN

Socotra
(Yemen)

Al Mukalla

Gulf of Aden

Equator

0

50°

RED

Sa'dah
San'a'

AFRICA

10°

0°

10°

20°

30°

40°

GEOGRAPHICAL WONDERS

Asia, the world's largest continent, has an enormous variety of landscapes. From some of the world's largest sandy deserts to crystal clear lakes and the highest summits in the world, it is truly a region of many contrasts.

Central Asia
Regions of wide desert and barren mountains dominate the landscape of Central Asia.

TURAN AND KAZAKHSTAN
DESERTIFICATION

Dry plateau

Central Asia is a region of hills, deserts and plateaus. In the middle of Central Asia sits the Aral Sea, the world's fourth-largest saltwater lake. Since 1960, it has shrunk by almost 75 per cent because the rivers feeding it were diverted to irrigate cotton fields. Poor vegetation, combined with the region's dry climate – less than 381 millimetres of rain a year – have contributed to the spread of a process called desertification. This is when an area of desert begins to replace land that was previously fertile.

CENTRAL ASIA
ALTAI MOUNTAINS

Asia Gold Range

The Altai Mountains stretch across parts of Russia, China, Mongolia and Kazakhstan. The mountains are separated by river valleys, which contain alpine meadows. The highest point is Mount Belukha (4506 metres), on which there are several glaciers. The region is home to many diverse species, including the snow leopard.

CHINA
YANGTZE RIVER

Three Gorges Dam

The River Yangtze is the third-longest river in the world after the Nile and the Amazon. Its source is in Tibet and it flows for 6300 kilometres before reaching the Yellow Sea. In the final stretch of its upper course lies the Three Gorges Dam. A monumental feat of engineering, this dam provides hydroelectric power to several large cities.

SAUDI ARABIA
DESERT SANDS

The Empty Quarter

South of the Arabian Peninsula is the Rub' al Khali Desert. The desert is one of the largest sandy deserts in the world and includes most of Saudi Arabia and areas of Oman, the United Arab Emirates and Yemen, covering 650,000 sq km. It is known for its extreme weather conditions, making it virtually impossible to cross.

SIBERIA
LAKE BAIKAL

The Blue Eye of Siberia
Lake Baikal is known as the Blue Eye of Siberia because its waters are so clear and blue. Containing 20 per cent of the world's unfrozen fresh water, the lake is 636 kilometres long and 1620 metres deep. In 1996, the lake became a UNESCO World Heritage Site.

Olkhon island
The island of Olkhon (below) is 730 square kilometres, and is the largest island of Lake Baikal in eastern Siberia. The island is covered with forests and a small steppe, in addition to its own lakes.

A view of Lake Baikal.

SOUTH-CENTRAL ASIA
THE HIMALAYAS

The Himalayas is the world's highest mountain range. It is 2440 kilometres long. The range includes the formidable Mount Everest, which has a summit of 8848 metres. The elevation of this mountain system is the result of a collision between the Indian and Eurasian tectonic plates, which began about 50 million years ago. The Himalayan region has many glaciers, which provide the area with a wealth of fresh water.

ASIAN RELIEF
ASIAN LANDSCAPE IN CROSS-SECTION

Asia has incredibly varied landscapes. As this cross-section shows, there are shields, deserts, plateaus and basins.

The weight of the Tibetan Plateau contributes to the expansion of the Earth's crust to the east and west.

The expansion of the Earth's crust has caused faults across the Tibetan Plateau.

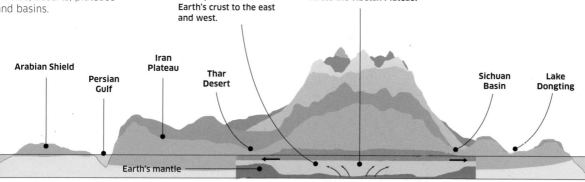

Arabian Shield · Persian Gulf · Iran Plateau · Thar Desert · Sichuan Basin · Lake Dongting · Earth's mantle

THE HIMALAYAS

The highest peaks on Earth, rising to nearly 9000 metres, are found in this Asian mountain range. The Himalayan mountain range extends across several countries, including Pakistan, India, Nepal, Bhutan and Tibet.

10,000

The number of attempts to climb Mount Everest in the last 50 years.

HIMALAYAN ORIGINS

Inhabitants of the heights

The inhabitants of the Himalayas belong to many different peoples who belong to different religious groups. Mongolians, who follow Buddhism, are found mainly in the north. Muslims are found in the south, east and west, with the centre of the region dominated by Hindus.

The first

On 29 May 1953, New Zealander Edmund Hillary and his guide Tenzing Norgay (below) became the first people to reach the summit of Mount Everest. It is possible that the Englishman George Mallory succeeded in 1924, but he died during the descent.

HIMALAYAN RANGE FACT FILE

Many chains

The Himalayas is a system composed of numerous mountain ranges.

Area covered by the chain:
612,000 square kilometres

Ecosystem:
High mountain

Maximum altitude:
Mount Everest 8848 metres

The nearest town

Muzaffarabad, the capital of Azad Kashmir, Pakistan, is located at the foot of the Himalayas. On 8 October 2005, a massive earthquake destroyed much of Muzaffarabad.

Flora

Firs, junipers (below), birch and rhododendron plants are widespread throughout the area.

Lake Tsomgo

Located at 3780 metres above sea level, Lake Tsomgo is 40 kilometres from Gangtok, the capital of the state of Sikkim. Although home to a variety of fauna and flora, the lake freezes over in the winter.

From space

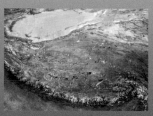

This satellite image shows the Himalayas as they look from space. The mountain range can be identified by the wrinkled appearance that it gives the Earth's surface.

RECORD
The Himalayan range has 10 of the 14 highest peaks on Earth.

The Sherpas

The valleys of the Himalayas are inhabited by the Sherpas. These people are used to life in the mountains and are often used as guides and escorts by mountaineers.

Mount Everest
The snowy peaks of the Himalayas rise high above the clouds.

MOUNT FUJI

This sacred mountain of Japan is a volcano that, while inactive for more than 300 years, is not extinct. It is considered to be the most perfect volcano on Earth because of the symmetry of its cone. At the base of Mount Fuji there are lakes, plateaus, waterfalls and caves.

Blue and white

The blue and white flycatcher is a migratory bird. It breeds in Japan, Korea and parts of China and Russia.

Spring

It is said to be spring in Japan when the cherry blossom tree comes into bloom.

TEMPERATURE
The lowest temperature ever recorded at Mount Fuji was -38 °C in February 1981.

Mount Fuji
Panoramic view of the volcano, the city Fujiyoshida and Lake Kawaguchi.

Lake Kawaguchi
This lake is very famous because it reflects the north face of Mount Fuji like a mirror.

Sea of Trees

The forest *Aokigahara Jukai*, or Sea of Trees, is found on the ruins left by an eruption that took place in AD 864.

From Tokyo

In this aerial view of Tokyo, you can see Mount Fuji, a symbol of Japan, in the background.

Technical details of Mount Fuji

Mount Fuji is located in central Japan, west of the capital Tokyo. It is an active volcano, but with little risk of eruption.

1. **Location:** Honshu Island

2. **Type:** Active stratovolcano

3. **Maximum altitude:** 3776 metres

Icy summit
The summit of Mount Fuji very seldom reaches above 0 °C.

Sacred spot

For centuries, Mount Fuji was considered so sacred that only monks and religious pilgrims climbed it. Until 1872, women were not allowed to climb it.

HISTORY
THREE ERUPTIONS

Mount Fuji
There have been three major eruptions of Mount Fuji, with each one adding to the shape and size of the volcano:

700,000 years ago: Komitake eruption. Its summit today overlooks the eastern slope of Fuji.

100,000 years ago: several eruptions of the Old Fuji. This was then covered by several more eruptions.

December 1707: the last eruption.

Actual Fuji

Old Fuji

Ashitaka (first volcano)

Komitake

TOURIST INFORMATION

Shiraito Falls

Although this waterfall has a drop of only about 20 metres, it is a Japanese national monument and is sacred to the Japanese. The falls are surrounded by trees, making them an attractive tourist destination.

THE MONSOON

Monsoons are seasonal winds that bring rains. They govern the life and economy of one of the most densely populated regions of the world. The monsoon season begins with heavy rains marking the end of the dry winter. Although people welcome the end of the winter, the monsoons can cause devastating floods that can destroy crops and homes.

ORIGIN
The word monsoon comes from the Arabic 'mawsim', which means 'season'.

Benefits from floods

Although the locals fear the flooding, the mud left by it increases soil fertility and ensures the health of future crops.

Crops in Oman

If monsoons do not destroy homes, they are welcomed by farmers because they make the soil more fertile, which leads to better crops.

Help from other countries

The devastating floods of 2010 left Pakistan reliant on help from other countries. Here, an observer in a military plane examines the scene of the floods.

2400
The number of deaths that occurred during the 2008 monsoon season.

Torrential rains
In Vietnam, in September 2009, torrential rains left 300 people homeless. Eight people were killed in the torrential rains.

India under water
In India, scenes like this are common during the monsoon season, which lasts from June to September.

Overflowing rivers

Rivers that join the mighty Ganges and the Brahmaputra in Bangladesh can be affected greatly by flooding rains, which devastate crops and property, and cause landslides.

HOW IT HAPPENS
MONSOON

Temperature differences

Monsoons are seasonal winds that vary in direction according to the season. The winter monsoon is a cold wind blowing from the continent to the ocean. The summer monsoon blows from the Indian Ocean and South China Sea into Asia, dragging with it warm and humid air. This wind crashes into the high mountains and causes heavy rains between April and October. In recent years, as a result of global warming and climate change, the monsoons have grown in intensity.

ASIAN MONSOONS
PAKISTAN-LADAKH-CHINA-KOREA

Devastation in 2010

Floods in Asia devastated large areas. In Pakistan, more than 300,000 homes were damaged or destroyed. In the region of Ladakh, India, at least 185 people died. In China, there were more than 700 deaths, and in North Korea, 800,000 people had to leave their homes.

Disaster in Pakistan
This aerial view shows the 2010 flooding in Muzaffargarh, southern Punjab, Pakistan. Around 14 million people lost their homes in the flood.

THE RIVER GANGES

The River Ganges has its source in the Himalayas, at 4140 metres. Along its 2506 kilometres course, it travels through mountains and plains to eventually empty into the Bay of Bengal. Civilizations have flourished on its banks, and today, cities, fertile rice paddies and temples are found along its banks.

City of 1000 temples

The Vishwanath temple is the holiest in Varanasi. Dedicated to the god Shiva, it is covered with 750 kilograms of gold.

GANGES BASIN
FACT FILE

Symbol of culture

The River Ganges is sacred to those who follow Hinduism. It also provides millions of people with fresh water.

Catchment area:
907,000 kilometres

Source of the river:
Gomukh at the mouth of Gangotri Glacier in the Himalayas

Length: 2506 kilometres

BELIEFS
RELIGIOUS CUSTOMS

The river is a goddess

For Hindus, the Ganges is personified as the goddess Ganga. Hindus believe it is important for them to bathe in the river and for the ashes of their deceased loved ones to be scattered on its waters.

The sacred river

The Ganges is sacred to followers of the Hindu religion. Its followers believe that the water of the river will save their souls. When Hindus die, they are cremated and their ashes are scattered in the river.

Varanasi, India
The city, seen from the river.

Contamination

Millions of people bathe in the River Ganges. All kinds of bacteria, sewage and remains of cremations are found in the river, making it a source of contamination.

1000
million
The number of litres of sewage found along the course of the river.

140 MILLION
There are 140 million people living in the Ganges Delta.

Suspension bridges

There are several bridges across the Ganges, including the Lakshman Jhula (which is older) and the Ram Jhula suspension bridges. They are designed only for pedestrians, but cyclists sometimes use them.

Calcutta (Kolkata)

With over 14 million inhabitants, Calcutta is one of the largest cities along the Ganges. During the colonial era, Great Britain ruled India. This building, dating from 1921, commemorates the British queen, Victoria.

ANIMALS OF THE GOBI DESERT

The Gobi Desert in northern China and southern Mongolia is extremely dry, especially during the winter. Extraordinary fossils have been found in the desert, which is home to camels, donkeys, wild horses, birds and reptiles.

A COLD PLACE
The Gobi Desert is cold and there is often frost on the dunes.

Small Gobi

In the area of Small Gobi (*Alashan*) in Mongolia, migratory birds build their nests in small shrubs.

Gobi bear

Persian gazelle

Bactrian camel

Asiatic wild ass

Mongolian cricket

Scorpion

Camel spider

Long-eared hedgehog

Long-eared jerboa

Mongolian gerbil

Powerful legs

The gerbil is active at night to avoid the high daytime temperatures. Gerbils use their strong hind legs and tails to leap in search of food, such as seeds.

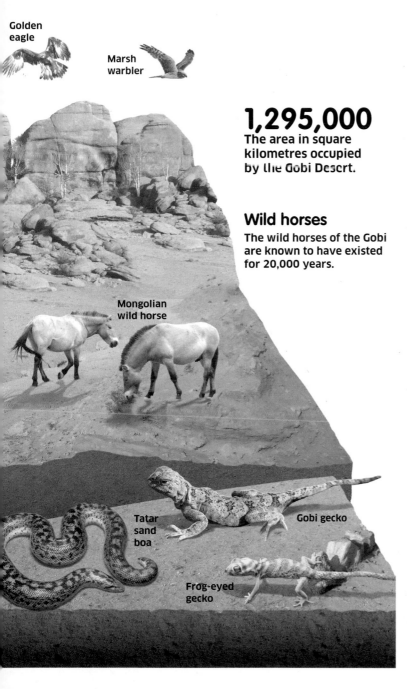

Golden eagle

Marsh warbler

1,295,000
The area in square kilometres occupied by the Gobi Desert.

Wild horses
The wild horses of the Gobi are known to have existed for 20,000 years.

Mongolian wild horse

Tatar sand boa

Gobi gecko

Frog-eyed gecko

Boa constrictors
Tatar sand boas are found in the Gobi Desert. These snakes hunt and kill their prey by squeezing it until it suffocates. Once the prey is dead, the snake then swallows it whole.

SPECIAL ANIMALS OF THE GOBI DESERT

Two-humped camels
Bactrian camels have two humps. They have adapted to the desert by growing a special coat, which helps them to withstand the extreme desert temperatures. In summer, it can reach more than 60 °C but in winter the temperature is often below 0 °C.

Herbivorous desert
Altai Nature Reserve is home to Persian gazelles (below), brown bears, wild horses and donkeys. The Persian gazelle can run quickly and cover up to 30 kilometres a day during winter. In the summer heat, they cover only 1 to 3 kilometres a day.

Fossils of the Gobi
The first fossils found in the Gobi were skulls of lizards and small mammals. Nests and fossilized eggs of dinosaurs have also been found. These fossils have helped scientists to understand how dinosaurs lived.

POPULATION AND ECONOMY

Although Asia has more people than any other continent, its population is not evenly distributed. Large uninhabited areas contrast with some of the most densely populated areas on the planet. The economy has huge inequalities. There are massive contrasts between the rich oil-producing and industrialized countries and the poverty of the countries in the central region.

Tokyo, Japan
A crowd of people on one of its streets.

POPULATIONS
THE MOST POPULATED

Beijing, China
China's capital city, Beijing, is home to about 19.6 million people. Among its attractions are the palaces of the Forbidden City and part of the Great Wall of China.

Calcutta (Kolkata), India
The state capital of West Bengal, Calcutta has an urban area that is home to over 14 million people. Its official name is Kolkata and, until 1911, it was the capital of India.

Tourism
Asia has many places for visitors to see and tourism contributes handsomely to the economy. These camels are taking tourists to the ruins of Petra in Jordan.

Rice paddies
Many Asian people still live in rural communities. Rice is the main agricultural product in Thailand. Rice grown there is exported around the world.

Rajasthan, India
Public transport
can be extremely
overcrowded
in India.

REGIONAL CONTRASTS
INFRASTRUCTURE

Transport
In wealthier Asian countries, with
growing or developed economies,
transport is highly developed.
For example, China has large
airports and rail systems. However,
in less economically developed
countries, transport is poor. For
example, in large parts of India
transport is scarce and unreliable.

Chinese wings
China Southern Airlines is
the leading airline in Asia.
Elephants are often used
as transportation in India.

HUMAN RIGHTS
CHILDREN

Poverty

Afghanistan, Bangladesh, Cambodia
and Laos are some of the poorest
countries in Asia. With little
economic development, people in
these countries have a shorter than
average life expectancy. In India and
Southeast Asia, more than 30 million
children are subjected to slave
labour in exchange for food.

PANORAMA
LOCAL VERSUS EXPORT

Industry in Asia

China and Japan are seen as
industrial powers. Many goods
are made in China and Japan and
exported to the West. While there
is massive industrialization in
parts of Asia, local industries, such
as handmade textiles, are still
important to some countries in Asia.

Kuwait
Oil has made
Kuwait one
of the richest
countries in the
Arabian Peninsula.

LANGUAGES AND PEOPLE

The size and diversity of the vast Asian continent mean that the people who live there are extremely varied. There are dozens of ethnic groups on the continent and most groups speak their own language.

Hangul

North and South Korea have the same alphabet, called the Hangul. It is made up of 24 consonants and vowels.

Religions

Islam, Buddhism and Hinduism are the main religions practised by the people of Asia.

MOST SPOKEN
Mandarin Chinese is one of the most widely-spoken languages in the world.

Monks reading religious texts in Tibet.

Paper and printing
Paper was invented in China in AD 104. Later in the 11th century, the Chinese were the first people to use a printing press.

Hebrew
The ancient language of Hebrew died in the 1st century AD. Nearly 2000 years later, it was revived and is spoken by almost all Israelis.

A COMPLEX HISTORY

Ancient civilizations
Some of the oldest civilizations in the world flourished in Asia. For example:

1 **Sumer (3200–2300 BC):** This civilization grew in today's Iraq. The Sumerians developed writing and mathematics.

2 **China (united from 221 BC):** The Chinese Empire flourished until 1912.

3 **Harappa (2600–1800 BC):** In the northwest of India, they developed a system of writing.

4 **Persia (550 BC):** The Persian Empire was centred around present day Iran

Islamic empires
After the rise of Islam, various empires formed:

1 **AD 630:** The tribes of the Arabian Peninsula were united in one state, which later expanded to include Syria, Palestine and Africa.

2 **1200–1300:** The Mongols of Central Asia started to follow Islam and formed an empire that included China and India.

3 **1300:** West Asian Turks created the Ottoman Empire, which controlled a large area until 1923.

European colonization
From the 15th century, the Portuguese began to trade and settle in parts of southern Asia. From the following century, the Dutch, English and French controlled trading posts and entire countries, such as India and Indonesia.

ETHNIC GROUPS
DIFFERENT LANGUAGES

MYANMAR
KAYAN

Long-necked women
Women of the Kayan people lengthen their necks by wearing long collars. With a population of just 130,000, the Kayan are one of Myanmar's ethnic minorities.

CHINA – VIETNAM – MYANMAR
MIAO

Living in the mountains
There are 7 million Miao people. They are found in the mountain regions of China, Vietnam and Myanmar. Their language is spoken in much of Southeast Asia.

FROM ASIA TO THE WORLD
ROMA

Mother and daughter
The Roma can be traced back to northwestern India to the states of Punjab, Gujarat, Rajasthan and Sindh (now Pakistan). Members of this group speak Romany.

INDIA
TODA

Pastoral people
Speaking a Dravidian language, this group lives in the Nilgiri Hills in southern India. They are shepherds and live in thatched houses built on wooden frames.

THE MONGOLS

Descended from the tribes led by Genghis Khan, the leader who conquered most of Eurasia in the early 13th century, the Mongols still live in the steppes of Asia, just as their ancestors did. Their lifestyle also remains largely unchanged and is still centred around their horses and grazing cattle.

FROM ASIA
THE BERING STRAIT

Across continents
Around 13,000–20,000 years ago, the Earth was approaching the end of the last glacial period. At that time, a small group of people ventured into northeastern Asia. They were probably in pursuit of game to hunt. The people crossed the Bering Strait, where the sea level was most likely lower than it is today. They had left Asia and arrived on the continent of North America in Alaska. The people eventually made North America their home.

A LARGE FAMILY

Asian and North American

Most scientists believe that the ancient Asians (their descendants are pictured below) who now inhabit southern Siberia are related to today's Native Americans.

Lunar New Year

Mongolians celebrate New Year according to the old lunar calendar. The festival is celebrated for three days in late January. People entertain guests and cook special food.

Traditional houses

Many Mongolians still live in large tents called yurts. The tents are easily transportable and suit the Mongolians' nomadic way of life.

Nomadic economy

Cattle give the Mongolians food in the form of meat and milk, transport and skins. Families travel great distances to find food for their cattle.

Hunting
A nomad on the steppes of Mongolia.

Culture

There are around 7-7.5 million Mongolians. Traditionally, they were hunters. Today, hunting is still an important part of their lives. They have a great spirit of cooperation and are usually very friendly with each other.

Beliefs

The Mongolian people have built shrines from rocks or wood, called oboo, in which they believe local spirits and gods live. Shrines usually face south or southeast.

Mongolian song and dance

Mongolians perform the *tsam* – a traditional masked dance to exorcize evil spirits. Mongolians play music on a variety of instruments and sing traditional songs.

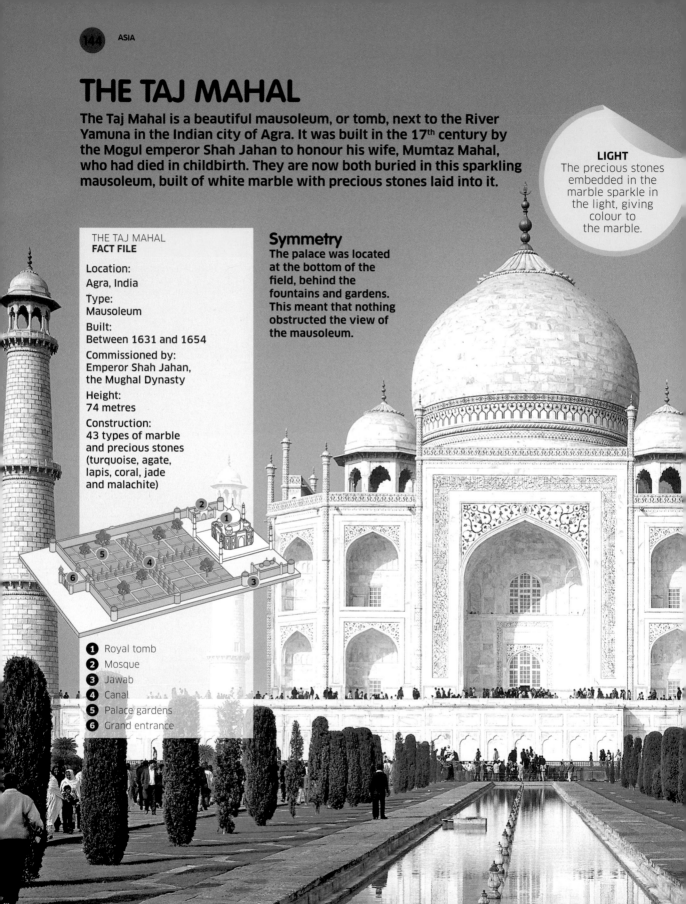

THE TAJ MAHAL

The Taj Mahal is a beautiful mausoleum, or tomb, next to the River Yamuna in the Indian city of Agra. It was built in the 17th century by the Mogul emperor Shah Jahan to honour his wife, Mumtaz Mahal, who had died in childbirth. They are now both buried in this sparkling mausoleum, built of white marble with precious stones laid into it.

LIGHT
The precious stones embedded in the marble sparkle in the light, giving colour to the marble.

THE TAJ MAHAL
FACT FILE

Location:
Agra, India

Type:
Mausoleum

Built:
Between 1631 and 1654

Commissioned by:
Emperor Shah Jahan, the Mughal Dynasty

Height:
74 metres

Construction:
43 types of marble and precious stones (turquoise, agate, lapis, coral, jade and malachite)

Symmetry
The palace was located at the bottom of the field, behind the fountains and gardens. This meant that nothing obstructed the view of the mausoleum.

1 Royal tomb
2 Mosque
3 Jawab
4 Canal
5 Palace gardens
6 Grand entrance

TAJ MAHAL **DETAILS**

Arches
The arches of each doorway give depth to the structure and reflect sunlight.

Borders
Drawing and verses from the Koran have been used to add decoration.

Onion-shaped dome
Domes of this shape are typical of Islamic architecture.

Minarets

Plinth
The mausoleum sits on a plinth. It adds height to the building, making it look more impressive.

Lattices
Filigree railings surround the area of the royal tombs.

Minarets
The tomb is surrounded by four towers, or minarets, one at each corner of the base. Faithful Muslims are called to prayer from the minarets.

22
The number of small domes symbolize the years of work.

Gardens
The gardens are divided into 16 sections, with many beds of flowers, raised paths, rows of trees, fountains, streams and wide ponds. The water reflects the majestic palace.

DETAIL
THE TOMBS

Features
Made of marble decorated with rhinestones, the tombs are found in the main building. They are decorated by a ring of lotus flowers. This decoration is repeated on each minaret.

Shah Jahan   Mumtaz Mahal

Burial chamber
The tombs of the couple are found in the central hall of the mausoleum.

BEIJING

The People's Republic of China's capital city, Beijing, is one of the world's most densely populated cities. The city is a mix of the ultramodern and the ancient, with skyscrapers and office towers sitting alongside ancient palaces, temples and plazas.

Dashalar
A view of this bustling shopping centre, just south of Tiananmen Square.

Country	China
Area	16,801 sq km
Population	19,612,000
Density	1167 people/sq km

CITY ICONS

Temple of Heaven

This round temple complex is typical of the buildings of the Ming Dynasty. Each morning in the temple grounds, people practise t'ai chi and qigong.

Tiananmen Square

Surrounded by public buildings, this is a large square in the centre of Beijing. It is the third largest public square in the world and has been the site of many events in Chinese history.

Dragon
The dragon is a symbol of force and power in Chinese culture.

SHOPPING
In this shopping avenue, shoppers can find everything, from modern jewellery and designer clothes, to traditional healers and medicines.

Entrance to Dashalar
Dashalar is a shopping avenue with more than 580 years of history. This bustling area gives an indication of what the ancient city of Beijing was like.

Transport

The city has a wide range of public transport which includes a subway, trains, buses, trams and aeroplanes. The image on the left shows Beijing Central Station.

Beijing National Stadium

The 2008 Olympic Stadium has been nicknamed the 'bird's nest' because of the intricate network of steel on its outside. The stadium is 330 metres long, 220 metres wide and 69 metres high.

CULTURAL EXPRESSIONS

National Grand Theatre

This building was designed by Paul Andreu and resembles an egg cut in half. The lagoon it rests on reflects the other half to make a complete oval. The theatre offers drama, dance and opera.

Beijing Opera

The Beijing Opera has two centuries of history. It is considered one of the highest forms of Chinese culture.

Population

Including the greater metropolitan area, the Beijing population is expected to reach 20 million by 2020.

THE FORBIDDEN CITY

Building of the Forbidden City in Beijing, China, began in 1406 during the Ming Dynasty. The city, with nearly 1000 buildings, took 14 years to complete. It was home to 24 emperors.

View of the museum Beijing, China.

Roofs
Pottery figurines of dragons and winged lions protect the Forbidden City from evil spirits.

THE FORBIDDEN CITY
FACT FILE

Date of construction:
1406–1420

Location:
Beijing, China

Features:
Covering 720,000 square metres, the city is surrounded by a moat that is 6 metres deep. Its thick walls are capable of withstanding gunfire.

Sahumadores

The palaces and courtyards had beautiful perfume burners, which spread a cloud of scent during ceremonies.

EXTREME SECURITY

The defences of the city
In addition to its thick walls and surrounding moat, the city has watchtowers at each of its corners. It was called Forbidden City because no one was allowed to enter or leave the city without permission from the emperor.

Ornamentation
Most of the buildings were built of wood. The ceilings have fine woodworked details on their eaves and numerous decorative pieces.

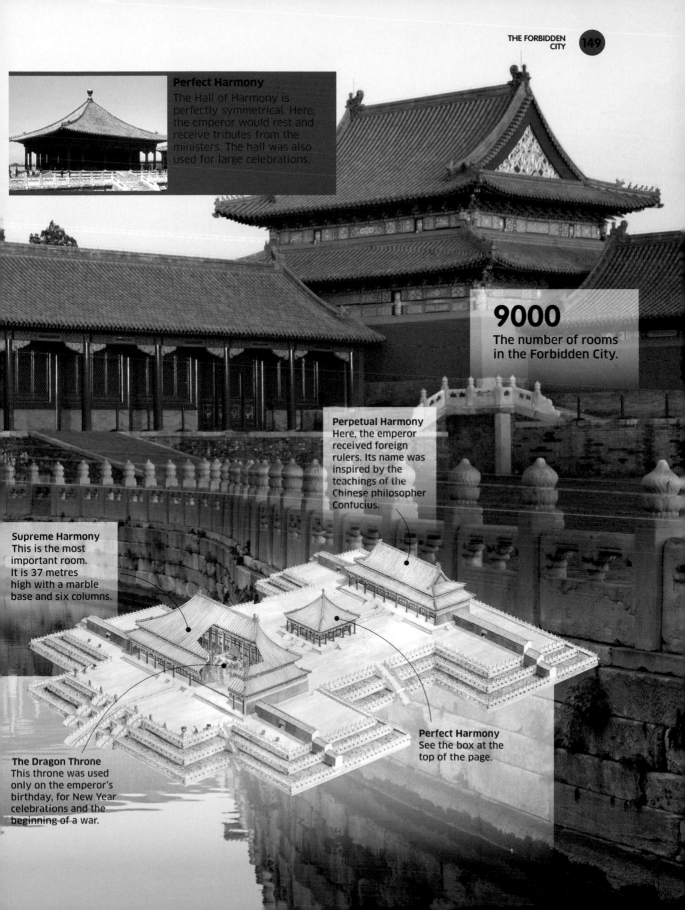

Perfect Harmony
The Hall of Harmony is perfectly symmetrical. Here, the emperor would rest and receive tributes from the ministers. The hall was also used for large celebrations.

9000
The number of rooms in the Forbidden City.

Perpetual Harmony
Here, the emperor received foreign rulers. Its name was inspired by the teachings of the Chinese philosopher Confucius.

Supreme Harmony
This is the most important room. It is 37 metres high with a marble base and six columns.

Perfect Harmony
See the box at the top of the page.

The Dragon Throne
This throne was used only on the emperor's birthday, for New Year celebrations and the beginning of a war.

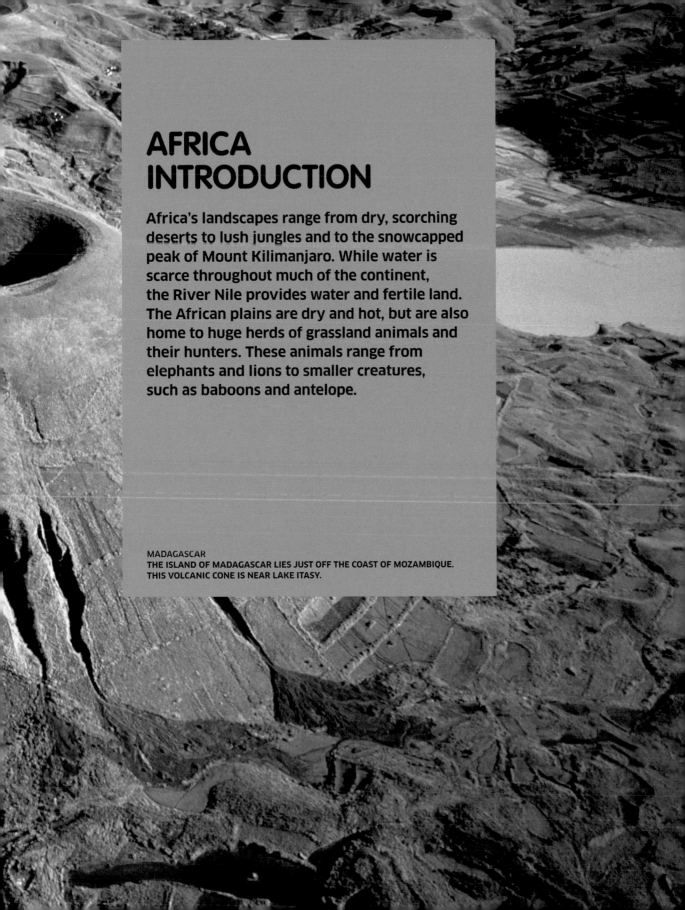

AFRICA
INTRODUCTION

Africa's landscapes range from dry, scorching deserts to lush jungles and to the snowcapped peak of Mount Kilimanjaro. While water is scarce throughout much of the continent, the River Nile provides water and fertile land. The African plains are dry and hot, but are also home to huge herds of grassland animals and their hunters. These animals range from elephants and lions to smaller creatures, such as baboons and antelope.

MADAGASCAR
THE ISLAND OF MADAGASCAR LIES JUST OFF THE COAST OF MOZAMBIQUE. THIS VOLCANIC CONE IS NEAR LAKE ITASY.

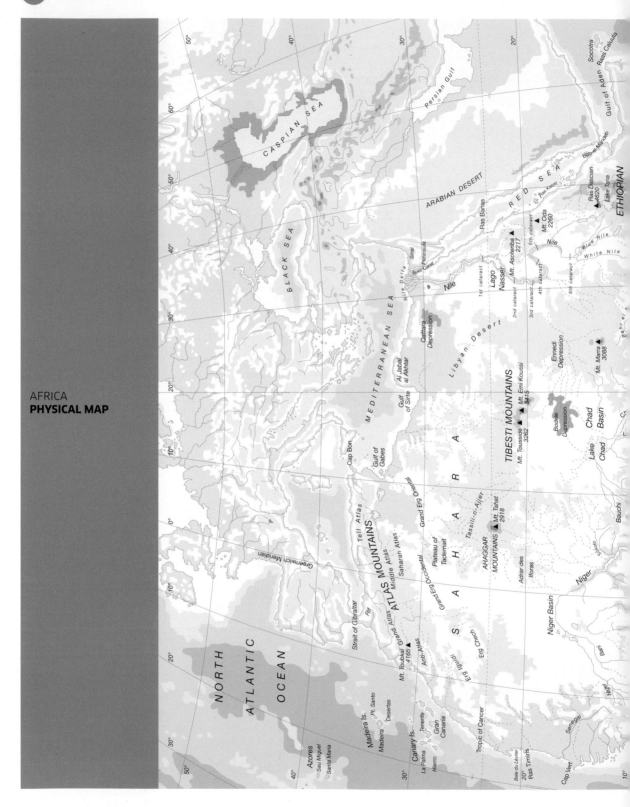

AFRICA
PHYSICAL MAP

NORTH

ATLANTIC

OCEAN

MEDITERRANEAN SEA

BLACK SEA

CASPIAN SEA

Persian Gulf

ARABIAN DESERT

RED SEA

Gulf of Aden

Socotra

Raas Caluula

Bāb el-Mandeb

Ras Kasar

Ras Dascian
4620

Lake Tana

ETHIOPIAN

Mt. Oda
2260

Blue Nile

White Nile

Nile

5th cataract

4th cataract

6th cataract

3rd cataract

2nd cataract

1st cataract

Mt. Asoteriba
2217

Ras Banas

Sinai

Suez Canal

Nile Delta

Nile

Lago
Nasser

Qattara
Depression

Libyan Desert

Ennedi
Depression

Mt. Marra
3088

Bahr el

Bodélé
Depression

Chad
Basin

Lake
Chad

TIBESTI MOUNTAINS

Mt. Emi Koussi
3415

Mt. Toussidé
3262

Al Jabal
al Akhtar

Gulf
of Sirte

S   A   H   A   R   A

Cap Bon

Gulf of
Gabes

Grand Erg Oriental

Plateau of
Tademaït

Tassili-n-Ajjer

Mt. Tahat
2918

AHAGGAR
MOUNTAINS

Adrar des
Iforas

Bauchi

Niger

Sokoto

Niger Basin

Bani

Tell Atlas

Grand Atlas

Middle Atlas

Saharan Atlas

ATLAS MOUNTAINS

Grand Erg Occidental

Erg Chech

Erg Iguidi

Anti-Atlas

Mt. Toubkal
4165

Rif

Strait of Gibraltar

Greenwich Meridian

Azores

Sāu Miguel

Santa Maria

Madeira Is.

Pt. Santo

Madeira

Desertas

Canary Is.

Tenerife

Gran
Canaria

La Palma

Hierro

Tropic of Cancer

Baie du Lévrier

Ras Timiris

Cap Vert

Senegal

Niger

60°

50°

50°

40°

30°

30°

30°

20°

20°

20°

20°

20°

10°

10°

10°

10°

10°

0°

0°

40°

40°

50°

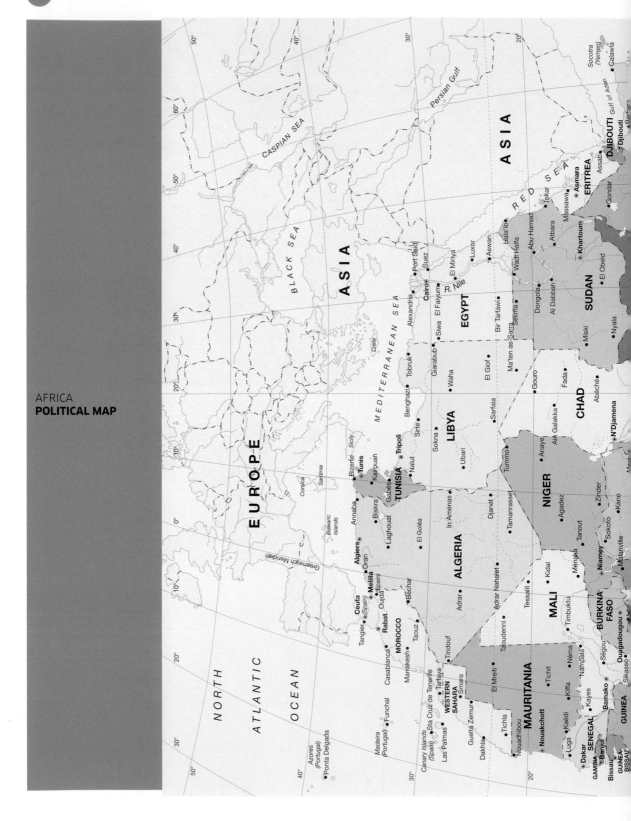

AFRICA
POLITICAL MAP

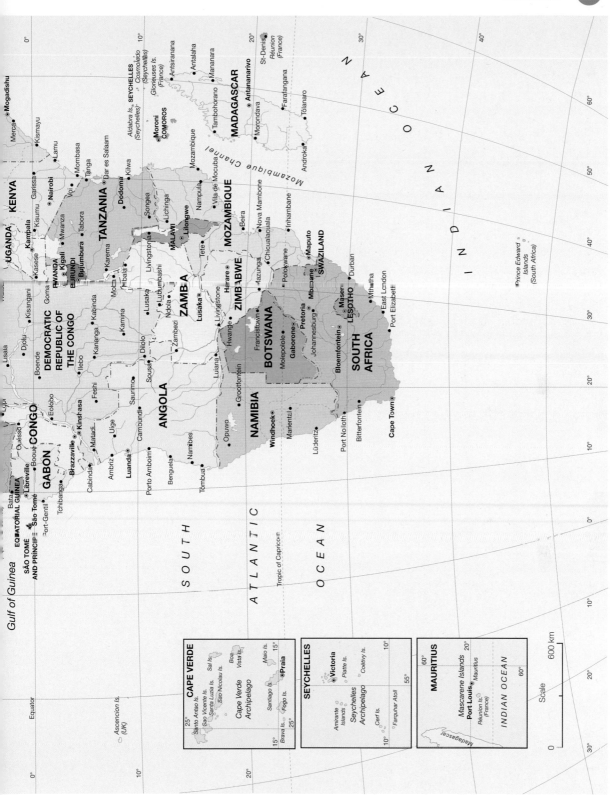

Gulf of Guinea

Mogadishu
Merca
Kismayu

UGANDA
KENYA
Kampala
Nairobi
Kaseses
Garissa
Kisumu
Voi
Mombasa
Lamu
Tanga
Dar es Salaam

RWANDA
Kigali
BURUNDI
Bujumbura
TANZANIA
Dodoma
Mwanza
Tabora
Songea
Karema

SEYCHELLES
Aldabra Is.
(Seychelles)
Moroni
COMOROS
Cosmoledo
(Seychelles)
Glorieuses Is.
(France)
Antsiranana
Antalaha
Mananara
MADAGASCAR
St-Denis
Réunion
(France)
Antananarivo
Tamboharano
Morondava
Farafangana
Tolanaro
Androka

Mozambique
Nampula
Lichinga
MALAWI
Lilongwe
MOZAMBIQUE
Tete
Beira
Nova Mambone
Inhambane

Mozambique Channel

Vila de Mocuba

DEMOCRATIC
REPUBLIC OF
THE CONGO
Djolu
Boende
Kisangani
Goma
Kabinda
Kananga
Kamina
Ilebo

Lusala
CONGO
Ouesso
Brazzaville
Kinshasa
Matadi

GABON
Libreville
Booué
Tchibanga

EQUATORIAL GUINEA
Bata
SÃO TOMÉ
AND PRINCIPE
São Tomé
Port-Gentil

Ascencion Is.
(UK)

ZAMBIA
Livingstonia
Lubumbashi
Karema
Mbala
Mbeya
Zambezi
Ndola
Lusaka
Livingstone
ZIMBABWE
Harare
Mazunga
Hwange

Kabinda
ANGOLA
Saurimo
Sousa
Grootfontein
Luiana
Dilolo
Cambúndi
Feshi
Uíge
Luanda
Ambriz
Porto Amboím
Benguela
Namibes
Tômbua
Cabinda

NAMIBIA
Windhoek
Opuwo
Mariental
Lüderitz
Port Nolloth
Bitterfontein

BOTSWANA
Francistown
Molepolole
Gaborone
Pretoria
Johannesburg
Bloemfontein
Polokwane
Maputo
SWAZILAND
Mbabane
LESOTHO
Maser
SOUTH
AFRICA
Durban
Mthatha
East London
Port Elizabeth
Cape Town

Chicualacuala

Prince Edward
Islands
(South Africa)

INDIAN OCEAN

SOUTH ATLANTIC OCEAN

Tropic of Capricorn

0°
10°
20°
30°
40°
50°
60°

Equator

CAPE VERDE
Santo Antão Is.
São Vicente Is.
Santa Luzia Is.
São Nicolau Is.
Sal Is.
Boa
Vista Is.
Maio Is.
Praia
Santiago Is.
Fogo Is.
Brava Is.
Cape Verde
Archipelago
25°
15°
25°
15°

SEYCHELLES
Victoria
Platte Is.
Coëtivy Is.
Amirante
Islands
Seychelles
Archipelago
Cerf Is.
Farquhar Atoll
10°
55°
10°

MAURITIUS
Mascarene Islands
Port Louis
Mauritius
Réunion Is.
(France)
Madagascar
INDIAN OCEAN
60°
60°
20°

Scale
0
600 km

GEOGRAPHICAL WONDERS

As a result of wind and water erosion, plateaus dominate the African landscape. The northern region is home to the Atlas Mountains. In the eastern region, the Great Rift Valley divides Africa from north to south.

A caravan of camels crossing the Sahara.

SAHARA
THE WORLD'S LARGEST DESERT

Temperature

The Sahara is the world's biggest desert, extending nearly 9 million square kilometres. Mountains, including the Ahaggar Mountains in southern Algeria (which have peaks of up to 3000 metres high), interrupt the desert landscape. The difference in temperature varies greatly between day and night. During the day, the temperature can reach above 50 °C; but at night it can drop to 0 °C.

TUNISIA – ALGERIA – MOROCCO
MOUNTAIN RANGES

Atlas Mountains

With peaks reaching more than 4000 metres, the Atlas Mountains in North Africa feature some of the highest peaks on the continent. The mountains run from east to west over 1500 kilometres and cross three countries.

ZAMBIA – ZIMBABWE
ZAMBEZI RIVER

Kariba Dam

In Africa, there are more than 1200 dams. Like the Kariba Dam, most of them were built as a solution to problems such as drought. Building these dams has caused serious damage to ecosystems and has led to a massive displacement of people.

DJIBOUTI – MOZAMBIQUE
GEOLOGICAL FRACTURE

Rift Valley

The Great Rift Valley is one of Africa's most important geographical features. It was formed 20–25 million years ago, when the Earth's crust broke along a stretch of weakness. It extends from western Asia to southeastern Africa.

KENYA
VOLCANIC MOUNTAINS

The last glaciers

There are only three glaciers left in Africa: Mount Kilimanjaro, Mount Kenya (left), which are both of volcanic origin, and Rwenzori Mountains. With the rapid increase in global warming, these glaciers are in serious danger of disappearing.

Old volcano

Mount Kenya was covered by ice for thousands of years. This has resulted in a badly eroded hillside and numerous valleys. It is now made up of 11 small glaciers.

Mount Kilimanjaro
An icy summit contrasts with the surrounding landscape.

ZAMBIA – ZIMBABWE
VICTORIA FALLS

Waterfalls

The Victoria Falls are located on the border between Zambia and Zimbabwe. The Falls are neither the world's highest nor widest. However, their height of 100 metres and their width of 1700 metres combined, make them the mightiest in the world. The Falls have been declared a World Heritage Site by UNESCO.

PROFILE
THE AFRICAN CONTINENT

This cross-section, from northwest to southeast, shows the great contrasts in the continent's relief.

5895 m
The height of Mount Kilimanjaro, Africa's highest mountain.

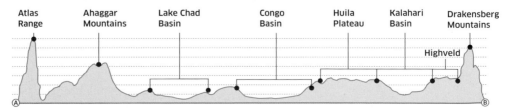

Atlas Range · Ahaggar Mountains · Lake Chad Basin · Congo Basin · Huila Plateau · Kalahari Basin · Drakensberg Mountains · Highveld

MOUNT KILIMANJARO

Africa's tallest mountain is a huge volcano that rises 5895 metres above sea level. Although Mount Kilimanjaro is only 330 kilometres south of the Equator, its summit remains covered with a layer of permafrost. The last volcanic activity on the mountain was just 200 years ago.

Elephants

Elephants, buffalo and giraffe can be found on the surrounding plains.

Glaciers

Mount Kilimanjaro's glaciers are shrinking as a result of global warming and possibly volcanic activity.

Three in one

Kilimanjaro has three craters: Kibo, Mawenzi and Shira. Mount Meru, in the Monduli Mountains, and Ngurdoto Crater lie to the west.

CRATERS OF KILIMANJARO

Monduli Mountains

Ngurdoto Crater

Mount Meru

Shira

Kibo

Mawensi

Technical data

Kilimanjaro is a stratovolcano located in Tanzania, East Africa.

1 Geological system: the Great Rift Valley which crosses from north to south.

2 Neighbouring ecosystems: forests and meadows.

3 Maximum altitude: Kibo Crater, 5895 metres.

40,000
The number of people visiting Kilimanjaro National Park each year.

Snowy peaks
An aerial view of Kilimanjaro.

A FASCINATING LANDSCAPE

POPULATION
DIFFERENT ETHNIC GROUPS

Daily life

The Chagga, Masai and Hadza are just three of the many ethnic groups that live near Mount Kilimanjaro. The Chagga people's livelihood depends on agriculture, and they grow bananas, yams (a type of tuber), beans and corn. The Masai are a semi-nomadic tribe that lives in northern Tanzania. They roam the plains raising cattle, sheep and goats. The Hadza (right) neither raise cattle nor do they grow crops. Instead, they forage the land as their ancestors did 10,000 years ago.

ROUTES OF ASCENT

Mountaineering and nature

Climbers of Mount Kilimanjaro do not need specific mountaineering experience to climb to the summit successfully, but they do need to be fit and healthy. Most people who climb the mountain do so with the help of a local guide. One of the biggest challenges for climbers is the altitude, which can cause headaches and breathing difficulties. Nearly one third of climbers fail to reach the summit. There are several routes to the summit, including Rongai, Machame and Marangu, which is the preferred route.

THE RIVER NILE

The legendary Nile in Egypt is the longest river in Africa and also in the world. (The River Amazon in South America is the largest river by volume of water.) The course of the river's flow of water makes parts of the desert habitable. Also, along the banks of the River Nile emerged one of the most important civilizations: ancient Egypt.

ELEVEN COUNTRIES
TRAVEL

Without borders

The River Nile runs through 11 countries: Egypt, Sudan, South Sudan, Democratic Republic of Congo, Rwanda, Uganda, Tanzania, Kenya, Ethiopia, Burundi and Eritrea. It crosses through deserts, forests, savannas, swamps and mountains. The Nile River Delta is one of the largest deltas in the world and, as a result of its fertile land, it is densely populated.

The big meeting

In the city of Khartoum, Sudan's capital, the White Nile from Uganda meets the Blue Nile, which flows from Ethiopia. These two tributaries flow together to form the River Nile.

DESCENT
From its source to its mouth, the Nile drops nearly 2000 metres.

95
The percentage of the Egyptian population that lives in the area of influence of the Nile.

6695 km
The length of the River Nile.

Satellite image of the River Nile Its huge delta flows into the Mediterranean.

DAMS
DYKES AND RESERVOIRS

Ecological damage

Since the late 19th century, many dams and reservoirs have been built on the Nile. These dams have caused great ecological damage. An example is the Aswan High Dam, built between 1960 and 1970 in Aswan, Egypt. The dam was seen as a way to ensure a permanent supply of water and a source of hydroelectric power. By damming the Nile, several river species have disappeared and the salt levels of the Delta's water have increased greatly.

Crocodiles

The Nile crocodile is a powerful predator, capable of killing a man.

Monuments

On both sides of the Nile stand great monuments, such as Luxor, the Valley of the Kings and the Pyramids of Giza.

FLORA AND FAUNA

Africa's rainfall is erratic and many parts of the continent experience regular droughts. Drought together with humankind's actions mean that many animal species, such as the gorilla and rhinoceros, are in danger of extinction.

Comoé National Park
This park lies in the Ivory Coast.

ISLAND OF MADAGASCAR
DIFFERENT SPECIES

Fossa

The fossa is found in the forests of Madagascar. Measuring from 80 to 90 centimetres long, this mammal can weight up to 10 kilograms. The fossa is quick and agile, catching its prey of lemurs and birds easily.

Hands of stone

Tsingy National Park is in the central west region of Madagascar. The park is home to various species of plant and animal, such as the lemur. The area is famous for its hard rock in the form of needles.

Gorillas

Hunting, mining and deforestation threaten the gorilla. Gorillas are found in forested areas, from Cameroon to the Democratic Republic of Congo.

Lemurs

The ring-tailed lemur is found in the wild only on the island of Madagascar. Lemurs feed on roots, leaves, fruit and insects.

Zebras
There are three
different species of
zebra found in Africa.

Palms

The desert vegetation of Africa has adapted to its environment. While shrubs, grasses and thorny plants grow in the desert itself, fruit, cereals and date palms flourish around oases. Date palms are especially useful to the people of the desert. Their leaves are used to provide shade and building materials for furniture, mats and baskets. The fruit is also eaten.

Baobab

The 'upside-down tree' or baobab is found in the semi-arid regions of sub-Saharan Africa. These trees can store up to 100,000 litres of water. The people of Africa use the tree in many different ways: rope and baskets are made from the bark fibre and the leaves and fruit are eaten. The fruit is very rich in vitamin C.

Master of the desert

Thanks to the camel's strength, these animals are used to carry loads across the desert as well as for farm work. They are also kept for their meat, wool and skins.

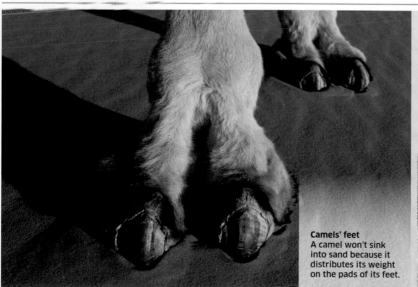

Camels' feet
A camel won't sink
into sand because it
distributes its weight
on the pads of its feet.

THE OKAVANGO DELTA

This extraordinary natural environment occupies 6 million hectares and has a rich biodiversity. After the summer rains, the Okavango River in Botswana swells and the rate of its water flow increases. The river flows to one of the driest areas of the world: the Kalahari Desert.

16,800 SQ KM

The surface area of the Okavango Delta.

HIPPO WARNING
Hippopotamuses open their mouths wide to display large fangs. They do this to intimidate their prey.

African jabiru

Hammerhead stork

Hippopotamus

African tiger fish

African pike

BETWEEN WATER AND LAND
The hippopotamus spends the daylight hours semi-submerged in water and the evening out to pasture. Hippos can eat 45 kilograms of plants in one night.

PAYBACK
Hippo dung provides nutrients for the aquatic plants. These plants are then fed on by fish, birds and crocodiles.

APPROPRIATE SUPPORT
The sitatunga antelope
has open hooves that are
specially adapted for
treading on soft ground.

Papyrus

Sitatunga

Wattled crane

Water lily

MARSHLAND
Water from heavy
rains in Angola
transforms arid land
into fertile swamp.

Nile crocodile

ADAPTATIONS
Wetlands are home to a great range of plants and animals. Mammals,
reptiles, amphibians, fish and insects are all found in wetlands. Wetland
animals are also adapted to dive into the water. For example, crocodiles have
nostrils, eyes and ears on top of their head, so they can breathe, hear and
see without leaving the water. Hippos can close their nostrils and slow their
heart rate down so much that they can stay underwater for half an hour.

**GIANT IN THE
OKAVANGO**

Elephants in the wild
The Okavango Delta is home to
many large herds of elephant.
In total, there are about 30,000
elephants in the region.

The animals form herds of females
and calves. The presence of
elephants is easy to recognize
because they often damage trees,
stripping the bark, which is left
behind on the ground.

AQUATIC PLANTS
TYPICAL EXAMPLES

Papyrus and water sprouts
Plants growing in the wetlands live
either entirely or almost entirely
submerged in water. Papyrus, water
lilies and water sprouts are the most
common plants in the habitat. Water
birds often walk on the plants in
search of food.

Crocodiles
The Nile crocodile is the largest
crocodile in Africa. It feeds on fish,
antelopes, zebras, buffalo and poultry.

THE AFRICAN SAVANNA

The African continent has the most extensive savanna in the world. Unlike the North American prairies, the African grasslands have shrubs and trees, such as acacias and baobabs. Many herbivore animals live together with their predators in this environment.

Giraffe

African elephant

African marabou

Wildebeest

White-backed vulture

Zebra

Termite

Termite mound

HERBIVORES AND PREDATORS

The savanna is home to many herbivores, grass and plant-eating animals, including buffalo, zebra, wildebeest, elephants, rhinoceros and giraffe. The predators found in the savanna are lions, leopards, cheetah and eagles. There are several different species of vulture, which are scavengers.

TERMITE SOCIETY

Termites are social insects like bees and ants. The members of each colony build a large nest made from their droppings, which contain sawdust. Inside the mound is a sophisticated network of tunnels to ensure the circulation of fresh air. The tunnels cannot be reached by predators.

ANIMALS
SCAVENGERS

Hyenas

The spotted hyena is found south of the Sahara, from Senegal and the Upper Nile to the southern tip of Africa. The hyena is known for its ungainly body. It scavenges on the prey remains of the big cats, for which it competes with vultures and jackals. In addition, hyenas are highly efficient hunters. To attack their prey, they use their powerful jaws. They also hunt as a pack, allowing them to prey on larger animals, such as zebra, giraffe and wildebeest.

Data file

Height:	70–90 centimetres
Weight:	40–70 kilograms
Gestation period:	110 days
Number of offspring:	2

Vultures

These scavengers are distinguished by their bald heads. By not having feathers on their heads, vultures can sift through the bloody remains of a kill without their heads becoming breeding grounds for parasites and disease. Vultures can have wingspans of up to 2.5 metres. In addition, they are able to hover in the sky using the air currents in search of prey.

Data file

Height:	95–110 centimetres
Weight:	up to 8.5 kilograms
Gestation period:	55 days
Number of offspring:	1

White rhinoceros

ACACIA
The acacia tree provides herbivores, such as giraffe, with food. Its wood is also especially strong

Lion

Scarab beetle

POPULATION

In Africa, the population is distributed according to each region's natural resources. For example, there are more people in the fertile coastal regions north and west of Nigeria, the Nile Valley and the eastern plateau. In recent decades, many people in rural areas have migrated to urban cities.

Cape Town
The urban sprawl of Cape Town on the mountainous coast of South Africa.

Nigerian children

The rate at which the population grows in Africa is high: the continental average is 2.3 per cent each year. Lagos in Nigeria is one of Africa's most populous cities.

Dakar

The site of the current capital of Senegal, Dakar, was first colonized by Europeans in the 15th century. The port is in a strategic position for maritime trade with both America and Europe. Today, it is one of the busiest ports in the world and is used to transport goods, such as chemicals, food and tobacco, from Mali and Mauritania.

EGYPT
CAIRO

An important city

Egypt's capital, Cairo, is located on the shores and islands of the River Nile. The city has theatres, universities and museums. Few places combine the past and present as Cairo does. On the streets of Cairo it is not uncommon to see carts pulled by donkeys next to expensive modern vehicles. Markets are crowded and the ringing of mobile telephones and public calls to prayer add to the hubbub of the markets.

REPUBLIC OF SOUTH AFRICA
JOHANNESBURG

Economic and financial centre

Johannesburg is the largest city in South Africa, one of the continent's wealthiest countries. The wealth stems from the rich gold, diamond and platinum mining industries. Johannesburg's city centre is home to 3 million people, but its metropolitan area is home to more than 7 million people. The majority of the population are black South Africans (73 per cent).

Kampala A street in the old city.

UGANDA
KAMPALA

HIV and malnutrition

The capital of Uganda, Kampala has a population of 1.6 million. The area has one of the highest rates of HIV infection. This reduces the productivity of families, which in turn increases the cases of malnutrition and orphaned children.

Street vendor In Uganda, more than half the population is under 15 years of age.

MOROCCO
MARRAKECH

Trade centre

The city of Marrakech was founded in 1062 by the Arabs. It became an important trading centre with the rest of Africa. Marrakech was a point of arrival and departure for merchants and the city's wealth attracted builders and craftspeople. Today, the city is known for its market, which offers a variety of goods, from traditional crafts to modern appliances.

PEOPLE AND LANGUAGES

With more than 3000 different groups of peoples in Africa, many have retained their identity by keeping their own language. Today, there are more than 2000 different languages spoken in Africa. The continent also has English, French and Arabic-speaking countries as a result of colonial times.

Most spoken

Arabic is one of the most widely-spoken languages in Africa. Other key languages include Swahili, Lingala and Bambara, as well as English, French, Portuguese and Spanish.

NOMADIC PEOPLE
In the 21st century, many people have held on to their own customs, such as the nomadic Tuareg from the north.

Education
Often, classes are held outside, such as this one in Makpandu, Sudan.

Papyrus

The papyrus plant that grows in the Nile Valley was used by ancient Egyptians to make paper. This invention means we now know about written history.

Muslims

After their conquests of the 7th century, the Arabs brought Islam to the territories of North Africa.

CULTURAL ISSUES
DIFFERENT HISTORIES

Four groups

Experts have divided the many African languages into four main families:

1 Afro-Asian (Arabic, Berber)
2 Niger-Congo (Bantu, Zulu)
3 Nilo-Saharan (Fur, Songhai)
4 Khoisan (Khoi, San)

Religions

There is a great variety of religions on the continent. Often, a religion blends two or more of these. For example:

1 Animism
2 Polytheism
3 Islam
4 Christianity

Great kingdoms

Many different civilizations formed powerful kingdoms that flourished on the continent. For example:

1 Egypt (3000–332 BC)
2 Ghana (800–1235)
3 Mali (1200–1600)
4 Benin (1500–1600)
5 Northern Arab Caliphates
  (641–1171)

European colonization

From 1884 to 1885, the European powers divided most of the continent into colonies. Although Spain, Germany and Belgium had their own colonies, most countries were colonized by:

1 France
2 Great Britain
3 Portugal

VARIETY
AFRICAN TRIBES

CAMEROON – CONGO – ANGOLA
BANTU

Villagers

A variety of peoples who speak Bantu languages have held on to their traditional customs and base their economy on agriculture.

CONGO
PYGMIES

Gatherers

Large populations of pygmy, or very small, people are found in the forested areas of the Congo. These people are gatherers.

KENYA – TANZANIA
MASAI

Semi-nomadic people

The life of the Masai revolves around raising cattle, sheep and goats. There are around 900,000 Masai on the continent.

DESERTS
BEDOUIN

Nomadic herders

The Bedouins of North Africa are Muslim and speak several dialects of Arabic.

THE SAN PEOPLE

The San, or Bushmen, are the native people of southern Africa.
Originally, they were found in South Africa, Zimbabwe, Lesotho,
Mozambique, Swaziland, Botswana, Namibia and Angola.
These people were traditionally hunter-gatherers, and today
their dwindling tribe is found mainly in the Kalahari Desert.

OUR PAST
WHAT MODERN SCIENCE TELLS US

Africa: starting point

According to modern genetic studies,
the San are the oldest living tribe.
It is believed that they are one of
the original tribes from whom all
others evolved. The San are
typically short people with light
skin and curly hair. A typical
member of the San tribe has a thick
layer of skin over the eyes, called
the epicanthic fold, which is also
characteristic of the peoples of
the East.

USING SOUND
TO COMMUNICATE

Peculiarity

The language spoken by the San
is characterized by its clicking or
popping sounds, a feature found in
the languages of other groups of
ancient African tribes.

Their dress

San men wear a triangular
loincloth, with the tip
passed between their legs.
The women wear an apron,
a hanging square in
front of a belt. They
also wear cloaks
over their
shoulders.

Kalahari Desert

The San are found in the
dry Kalahari Desert. They
obtain food by hunting
animals and gathering
plants. Some San have
found work as shepherds.

Water collection

To survive, the San have to be able to find water. They suck water from plant roots and empty ostrich eggs. This image (left) shows an ostrich egg next to a hen's egg.

Hunters
San men hunt alone or with their children using bows and arrows. Their arrows are dipped in poison, which they get from poisonous snakes.

Kalahari Desert
San children and a woman sit around a camp fire.

Tradition of fire
San people would traditionally light a fire by turning a stick on soft wood.

Houses

San shelters are made by the women wherever there is vegetation. When their food supply runs out, the group will move to another area.

Art
San cave paintings are some of the oldest in the world. Their paintings often tell a hunting story. This example (left) is found in a cave in Murewa, Zimbabwe.

ECONOMIC RESOURCES

Africa may often appear to lack wealth. However, its natural resources offer huge potential wealth. The continent has the greatest sources of precious stones and metals in the world. South Africa has some of the richest companies and industries on the continent.

Marrakech market
Every day, thousands of people visit the market, filled with crafts and other products.

AFRICAN ART
DIFFERENT TRADITIONS

Features

Because of very different traditions, African art often reflects its mixed heritage. It includes wooden sculptures, masks and crafts in metal and other materials.

Lamp
A traditional North African lamp made from brass and stained glass.

KENYA
FARMING

Subsistence and export

There are two types of farming on the African continent. The first is called subsistence farming. Here, a farmer will work small areas of land, growing just enough food for the farmer and the immediate family. The second type of farming is large-scale agriculture for the export of crops. This type of farming now occupies nearly 40 per cent of land that is suitable for farming. It consists of large plantations, often owned by foreign companies. The most common crops grown include cocoa, bananas, coffee and tea.

TOURISM
SAFARIS

Most visited

Tourism provides a great source of income for the continent. Many visitors go on safari in Kenya and Tanzania to see African wildlife in its natural habitat.

A tea picker in Kenya.

In the Sahara
Goats provide a good source of food in desert areas.

FISHING

Consuming local food

Africa has rich resources of fish. A good source of food, most fish caught is eaten locally. Only Morocco, Senegal, Ivory Coast, South Africa and Namibia are countries rich enough to be able to export their fish. The Great Lakes region has many amazing freshwater fish, too. Countries such as Tanzania, Uganda, Kenya and Nigeria catch these freshwater fish.

FOREST

Timber production

In recent years, African forests have been in danger from people who have begun to cut down a large number of trees. Areas of forest that are near to sea ports or larger local markets have lost the greatest numbers of trees.

In the Central African Republic, for example, between 15 and 18 different types of tree are being cut down, while in the Democratic Republic of Congo, 18 to 20 species are disappearing. Many environmental groups fear that these actions will destroy the habitats of many species of animal, especially the gorilla whose numbers are dwindling.

A lumberjack cutting a tree with a chainsaw.

DIFFERENT OPPORTUNITIES

Peasant women

Around 70 per cent of farm work in the region is done by women. However, most of the income from agriculture is controlled by men. This tradition has led to great inequalities between men and women in their households.

CAIRO

Located on the River Nile, Cairo is the largest city in the Arab world and Africa. Rich in ancient monuments, theatres and museums, this historic centre was declared a World Heritage Site by UNESCO.

Country	Egypt
Area	453 sq km
Population	7,010,000
Density	15,475 people/sq km

CITY EMBLEMS

The Alabaster Mosque

Built between 1830 and 1848, this mosque consists of a central dome surrounded by four others, and has two equal minarets that stand 82 metres tall. Below, you can see the front and inside of the building.

The Cairo Tower
Located in the Zamalek district, this television tower is 187 metres tall. On the 14th floor there is a revolving restaurant.

Mosque of Al-Azhar

This mosque was dedicated in 972. Its name means 'the most splendid'.

Madrasa al-Taybarsiyya

Originally designed to complement the mosque of Al-Azhar, the Madrasa al-Taybarsiyya was built in 1309. It houses the tomb of Prince Amir Taybars.

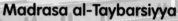

Mosque of Al-Azhar
The mosque is in the centre of the city.

Street fairs

The souk, or market, of Cairo is a maze of narrow streets and tiny shops filled with goods of all kinds, such as slippers, scarves, glass pipes, spices or jewellery.

The Egyptian Museum

This museum holds the greatest collection of objects from ancient Egypt, and has more than 120,000 pieces. Over 2.5 million people visit the museum every year.

Minaret Qaitbay

Built in 1483, this cylindrical tower has three balconies and arched panels. It was from these towers that the call to prayer came.

Egyptian sweets

Egyptian bakeries are famous for their delicate sweets, which are made of almonds, honey, cereals and grits (a type of corn).

A THOUSAND MINARETS
Cairo is known as the city of 'the thousand minarets', which refers to the number of mosques in the city.

Religion

The majority of the city's population are Muslim. These girls are wearing traditional Muslim veils.

Demography

The inhabitants are mostly descendants of the ancient Egyptians, Arabs, Bedouins and Berbers.

THE PYRAMIDS OF GIZA

Opposite the city of Cairo, across the River Nile, the mighty pyramids of Giza rise majestically. Built 4500 years ago, the pyramids house the tombs of the pharaohs Khufu, Khafre and Menkaure. They are the greatest symbol of the culture of ancient Egypt.

MAP OF THE VALLEY OF THE KINGS

Location

The valley is home to the three most famous Egyptian pyramids: Khufu, Khufu's son, Khafre, and Menkaure. The map below shows how the complex was laid out.

1. Pyramid of Khufu
2. Pyramid of Khafre
3. Pyramid of Menkaure
4. Great Sphinx
5. Great Temple
6. Procession route
7. Tomb of a dignitary
8. Mortuary temple
9. Secondary pyramid

The Great Sphinx
Carved from a single rock, it has the body of a lion and a human face.

2,521,000 cubic m

The total volume of the pyramid of Khufu.

Gold peak

The white limestone at the top was covered with a shiny metal, possibly gold.

Khufu

Two million stones, each weighing 200 kilograms, were used to build this pyramid. The pyramid is the same height as a 40-storey building.

Small pyramids

East of the pyramid of Khufu, three other smaller pyramids were found.

Ramp system

No one is sure quite how the
pyramids were built, but it is
known that large blocks of
stone were loaded using
a complex system of ramps.

Possible ramp methods

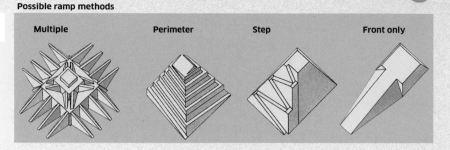

Multiple   Perimeter   Step   Front only

Khafre

The pyramid of Khafre
is guarded by the Great
Sphinx, a symbol of the
pharaoh.

Destination

The pyramids were built to
protect the dead pharoah's
body. Khufu's pyramid
took 33 years to build.

VILLAGE
Near the Sphinx,
there was a town where
officials and the workers
responsible for the
construction of the
pyramids lived.

Menkaure

In Menkaure's burial
chamber, an empty
sarcophagus (stone
coffin) was found.

Spectacular sight
The pyramids
at sunset.

OCEANIA INTRODUCTION

Oceania is the world's smallest continent and includes Australia, New Zealand, Papua New Guinea and many Pacific islands, including Micronesia, Fiji, Tonga and Samoa. Before European explorers visited Oceania, the region was occupied by native people, such as the Maori. English, French, Dutch and Portuguese people settled there, creating colonies. Many of these colonies are now independent, with their own lifestyles and cultures.

CAMPBELL ISLAND, NEW ZEALAND
THE ISLAND REMAINS UNINHABITED. THE FEW PEOPLE TO REACH ITS
SHORES ARE USUALLY SCIENTISTS WHO STUDY WILDLIFE FOUND THERE.

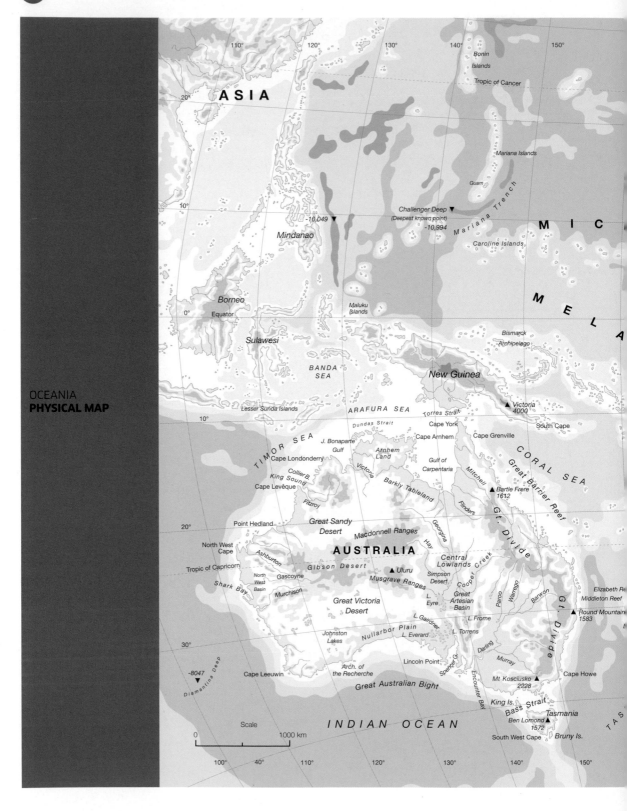

OCEANIA
PHYSICAL MAP

110° 120° 130° 140° 150°

Bonin
Islands

Tropic of Cancer

20°

ASIA

Mariana Islands

Guam

M I C

10°

Challenger Deep ▼
(Deepest known point)
-10,994

Mariana Trench

-10,049 ▼

Mindanao

Caroline Islands

0°   Equator

Borneo

Maluku
Islands

M E L A

Sulawesi

Bismarck
Archipelago

BANDA
SEA

New Guinea

Lesser Sunda Islands

ARAFURA SEA

Torres Strait

▲ Victoria
4000

10°

Dundas Strait

Cape York

South Cape

Cape Arnhem

Cape Grenville

TIMOR SEA

J. Bonaparte
Gulf

Arnhem
Land

Cape Londonderry

Collier B.
King Sound
Cape Levêque

Victoria

Barkly Tableland

Gulf of
Carpentaria

Mitchell

CORAL SEA

Great Barrier Reef

▲ Bartle Frere
1612

Fitzroy

Flinders

Gt. Divide

Point Hedland

Great Sandy
Desert

Macdonnell Ranges

Georgina

Hay

20°

North West
Cape

Ashburton

AUSTRALIA

Central
Lowlands

Tropic of Capricorn

North
West
Basin

Gascoyne

Gibson Desert

▲ Uluru
Musgrave Ranges

Simpson
Desert

Cooper Creek

Paroo

Warrego

Barwon

Elizabeth Re
Middleton Reef

Shark Bay

Murchison

Great Victoria
Desert

L.
Eyre

Great
Artesian
Basin

L. Frome

▲ Round Mountain
1583

L. Gairdner

Gt. Divide

L. Everard

L. Torrens

30°

Johnston
Lakes

Nullarbor Plain

Darling

Murray

-8047 ▼

Arch. of
the Recherche

Lincoln Point

Spencer G.

Cape Howe

Diamantina Deep

Cape Leeuwin

Great Australian Bight

Encounter Bay

Mt Kosciusko ▲
2228

King Is.

Bass Strait

TAS

Scale

INDIAN OCEAN

Ben Lomond ▲
1572

Tasmania

0   1000 km

South West Cape

Bruny Is.

100° 40° 110° 120° 130° 140° 150°

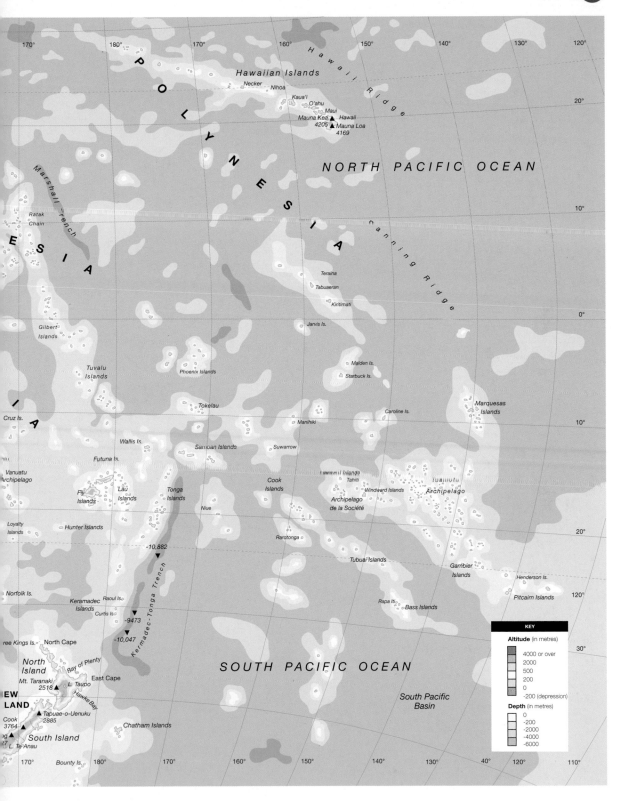

P O L Y N E S I A

Hawaii Ridge

Hawaiian Islands
Necker Nihoa
Kaua'i
O'ahu
Maui
Mauna Kea ▲ Hawaii
4205 ▲ Mauna Loa
4169

NORTH PACIFIC OCEAN

Marshall Trench

Ratak
Chain

Fanning Ridge

10°

20°

ESIA

ESIA

Teraina
Tabuaeran

Kiritimati

0°

Gilbert
Islands

Jarvis Is.

Malden Is.
Starbuck Is.

Tuvalu
Islands

Phoenix Islands

Marquesas
Islands

Caroline Is.

10°

Cruz Is.

I
A

Tokelau

Manihiki

Wallis Is.

Samoan Islands

Suwarrow

Futuna Is.

Vanuatu
Archipelago

Fiji
Islands

Lau
Islands

Tonga
Islands

Niue

Cook
Islands

Leeward Islands
Tahiti

Windward Islands

Tuamotu
Archipelago

20°

Loyalty
Islands

Hunter Islands

Archipelago
de la Société

Rarotonga

-10,882

Tubuai Islands

Gambier
Islands

Henderson Is.

120°

Norfolk Is.

Keramadec
Islands Raoul Is.
Curtis Is.

Kermadec-Tonga Trench

-9473

Rapa Iti
Bass Islands

Pitcairn Islands

-10,047

ee Kings Is. North Cape

North
Island

Bay of Plenty

East Cape

30°

SOUTH PACIFIC OCEAN

Mt. Taranaki ▲
2518

L. Taupo

Hawke Bay

EW
LAND

Cook
3764 ▲

Tapuae-o-Uenuku ▲
2885

South Island

Chatham Islands

South Pacific
Basin

L. Te Anau

170° Bounty Is. 180° 170° 160° 150° 140° 130° 40° 120° 110°

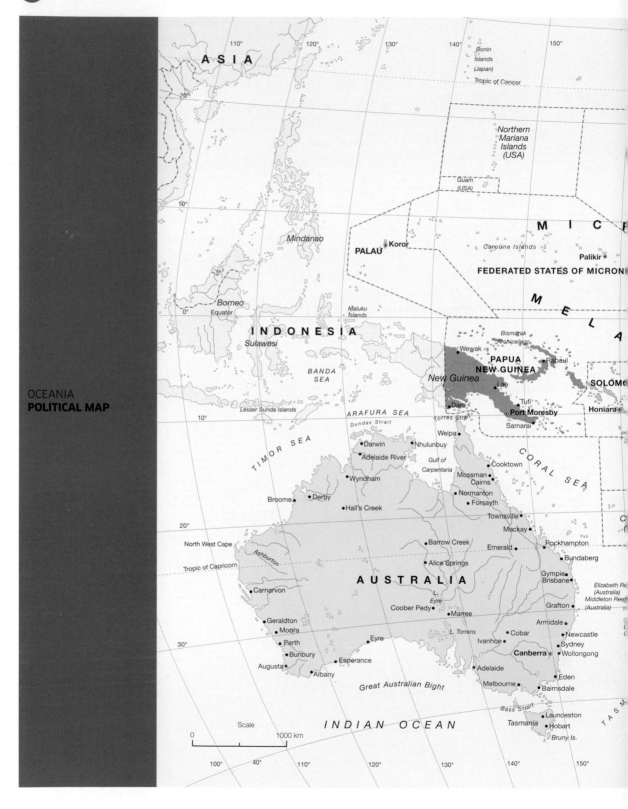

OCEANIA
POLITICAL MAP

ASIA

110° 120° 130° 140° 150°

Bonin
Islands
(Japan)

Tropic of Cancer

20°

Northern
Mariana
Islands
(USA)

10°

Guam
(USA)

M I C R

Mindanao

PALAU • Koror

Caroline Islands

Palikir •

FEDERATED STATES OF MICRON

0° Equator

Borneo

Maluku
Islands

M E L A

I N D O N E S I A

Sulawesi

Bismarck
Archipelago

• Wewak

PAPUA
NEW GUINEA

• Rabaul

BANDA
SEA

New Guinea

• Lae

SOLOMO

Lesser Sunda Islands

10°

ARAFURA SEA

Dundas Strait

• Daru

• Tufi

• Port Moresby

Honiara •

Torres Strait

• Samarai

Weipa •

T I M O R   S E A

• Darwin

• Nhulunbuy

• Adelaide River

Gulf of
Carpentaria

• Cooktown

C O R A L   S E A

• Wyndham

Mossman •
Cairns •

Broome • • Derby

• Normanton

• Hall's Creek

• Forsayth

Townsville •

20°

Mackay •

North West Cape

• Barrow Creek

Emerald •

• Rockhampton

Ashburton

• Bundaberg

Tropic of Capricorn

• Alice Springs

A U S T R A L I A

Gympie •
Brisbane •

Elizabeth Re
(Australia)
Middleton Reef
(Australia)

• Carnarvon

L.
Eyre

Coober Pedy •
• Marree

• Grafton

Armidale •

• Geraldton
• Moora

L. Torrens

• Cobar

• Newcastle

30°

• Perth

Ivanhoe •

• Sydney

• Eyre

Canberra

• Wollongong

• Bunbury

• Esperance

Augusta •

• Albany

• Adelaide

• Eden

Great Australian Bight

Melbourne •

• Bairnsdale

Bass Strait

• Launceston

Scale

Tasmania

• Hobart

I N D I A N   O C E A N

• Bruny Is.

T A S M

0   1000 km

100° 40° 110° 120° 130° 140° 150°

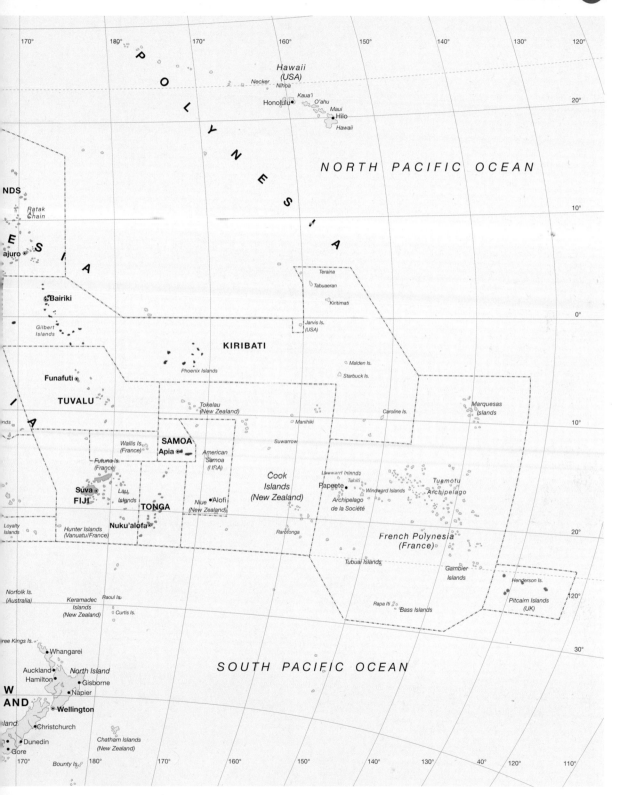

170°   180°   170°   160°   150°   140°   130°   120°

P O L Y N E S I A

Hawaii
(USA)

Necker
Nihoa

Kaua'i O'ahu
Honolulu●   Maui
●Hilo
Hawaii

NORTH PACIFIC OCEAN

20°

10°

NDS

Ratak
Chain

E S I A

ajuro ●

Bairiki

0°

Teraina
Tabuaeran

Kiritimati

Gilbert
Islands

KIRIBATI

Jarvis Is.
(USA)

Malden Is.
Starbuck Is.

Funafuti ●

Phoenix Islands

Marquesas
Islands

TUVALU

Tokelau
(New Zealand)

Caroline Is.

10°

Manihiki

I A

Wallis Is.
(France)

SAMOA
Apia ●●

Suwarrow

Futuna Is.
(France)

American
Samoa
(USA)

Cook
Islands
(New Zealand)

Leeward Islands
Papeete ● Tahiti

Tuamotu
Archipelago

Suva ●
FIJI

Lau
Islands

TONGA

Niue ● Alofi
(New Zealand)

Windward Islands

Archipelago
de la Société

French Polynesia
(France)

20°

Loyalty
Islands

Hunter Islands
(Vanuatu/France)

Nuku'alofa ●

Rarotonga

Tubuai Islands

Gambier
Islands

Henderson Is.

120°

Norfolk Is.
(Australia)

Keramadec
Islands
(New Zealand)

Raoul Is.

Curtis Is.

Rapa Iti ●
Bass Islands

Pitcairn Islands
(UK)

ree Kings Is.

● Whangarei

30°

Auckland ●
Hamilton ●

North Island

SOUTH PACIFIC OCEAN

● Gisborne
● Napier

W
AND

● Wellington

land

● Christchurch

Chatham Islands
(New Zealand)

● Dunedin
● Gore

170°   180°   170°   160°   150°   140°   130°   40°   120°   110°

Bounty Is.

GEOLOGY AND LANDSCAPE

Originally, Oceania and Antarctica were one landmass called Gondwana. As a result of continental drift, lands split apart into the many volcanic islands and coral reefs that are found in the Pacific Ocean today.

Blue Mountains Australia's Blue Mountains have been declared a Natural Heritage Site by UNESCO.

Three Sisters

These rock formations are found in the Blue Mountains in the Australian state of New South Wales. Each 'sister' is just over 900 metres high. They were formed when the sandstone eroded.

Tongariro and its holy sites

Tongariro on the North Island is New Zealand's oldest national park. It holds a great spiritual importance for the original inhabitants of New Zealand, the Maori. The park has three active volcanoes, which add to its natural beauty. Visitors to the park can walk along the many trails, and for the more adventurous there is white-water rafting.

Arthur's Pass, New Zealand

Arthur's Pass is the highest pass over New Zealand's Southern Alps. It is named after Arthur Dudley Dobson, who found his way over the pass in 1864, but the route was already known to the Maori. The highest peak in the Southern Alps is the 2400-metre-high Mount Murchison. Popular activities include rock climbing, mountain biking and hiking.

GEOGRAPHY AND CLIMATE
THE WORLD'S SMALLEST CONTINENT

Great Eastern Ranges, Australia

The Great Dividing Range (above) is the third-longest mountain range in the world. It stretches almost the entire length of Australia's east coast. The highest peak in the country, the 2228-metre-high Mount Kosciusko (left) is found here.

Great Barrier Reef
Off the coast of northeastern Australia, the Great Barrier Reef is the largest living coral reef in the world.

SEAS AND VOLCANOES
POLLUTION WATCH

Timor Sea

Located between the island of Timor and Australia, the Timor Sea borders the Indian Ocean. In 2009, there was a major oil spill there, which had a disastrous effect on birds, marine invertebrates, coral and algae.

Mount Egmont, New Zealand

Called Taranaki by the Maori, Mount Egmont is a dormant volcano, 2518 metres high. The volcano was last active in 1655. Other active volcanoes on the North Island include Ruapehu, Ngauruhoe and Tongariro.

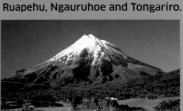

Uluru
Found in central Australia, this red sandstone rock is sacred to the Aboriginal people of the area.

AUSTRALIA
ULURU

Sacred rock

Located in Australia's Northern Territory, Uluru is just one of the attractions of the Uluru-Kata Tjuta National Park. This giant red rock stands 348 metres high. Considered one of the most important sites in Aboriginal culture, the rock is frequently visited by Aboriginals for ceremonies and rituals.

FLORA AND FAUNA

Some exotic plants and animals came to Oceania with the arrival of foreign explorers and settlers. However, Australia still has many species that are found nowhere else, including the kangaroo, the Tasmanian devil and the koala bear.

Lupins
These striking plants were brought to New Zealand by settlers from Europe.

PROTECTED SPECIES
LIVING FOSSILS

Reptile

The tuatara lizard is found in New Zealand. Its name means 'spiny back' in Maori. It grows to 70 centimetres long and is considered a living fossil because it is not found anywhere else on the planet.

EXOTIC SPECIES
NOW A PEST

Mynah bird

The mynah bird is native to Asia. It was introduced to the region by the British to control crop pests. Today, this bird is considered to be a pest in both rural and urban areas and is a threat to the native bird species of Oceania.

MOVIE MAGIC
FINDING NEMO

Clownfish

Clownfish live in the Pacific Ocean. Easily recognized by their bright orange colour, clownfish are carnivorous and live with sea anemones on the coral reefs of the Pacific.

Frigatebird

The frigatebird is a symbol on the flag of the island nation of Kiribati. It is easily identified by its swollen red throat.

BIRD OF PARADISE
The bird of paradise is the national bird of Papua New Guinea.

Brown booby

The brown booby bird is found along the coastlines of Tuvalu, Micronesia, French Polynesia and Australia. Brown boobies eat mainly small fish or squid that gather in groups near the surface of the ocean.

Surgeonfish

Diversity

There are 1500 species of fish and 2200 plant species living on the Great Barrier Reef.

Angelfish

Butterflyfish

Tasmanian devil

The Tasmanian devil is an aggressive carnivorous marsupial. It is found only on the island of Tasmania, off the coast of southern Australia.

Koala

This plant-eating marsupial grows up to 75 centimetres long.

Saltwater crocodile
The saltwater crocodile is the largest and most dangerous crocodile in the world.

Kiwi

The kiwi bird is the official symbol of New Zealand. The kiwi is a very rare bird that is active mainly at night. Kiwi birds cannot fly because their wings are too small.

Eucalyptus
The Eucalyptus is the most common native tree in Australia.

POPULATION AND ECONOMY

Australia and New Zealand are the largest countries in Oceania, but they have some of the lowest population densities. These two countries have developed and stable economies with strong trade links to Southeast Asia. Many of the smaller countries and colonies in Oceania struggle to get by on income from tourism and agriculture.

Sydney, Australia
Pedestrians cross between George Street and Park Avenue, in the heart of the city.

NEW ZEALAND CITIES

Auckland
The largest city in New Zealand, Auckland has two ports. It is also the economic and cultural centre of the country.

Government
In 1893, New Zealand became the first country in the world to recognize the right of women to vote. While some colonies are fighting for independence, most countries in the region are democracies.

Boat taxis
These are used by the people of Micronesia to get around. They are also rented out to tourists visiting the islands.

Australian industry
Australia is the most advanced country in the region. It has large chemical, petrochemical, food and drink industries.

New Zealand
This country is one of the largest sheep farming nations in the world.

CONTRASTING INFRASTRUCTURE

Houghton Highway

The longest bridge in Oceania is the Houghton Highway in Queensland, Australia. This viaduct is 2740 metres long. While Australia has 812,972 kilometres of road, Tuvalu has just 8 kilometres. Most countries in the region trade by sea.

Wine industry
Australia is a large producer of wine. It is the fourth largest exporter of wine in the world.

City link
The Sydney monorail runs through the city.

RICHNESS OF PEOPLE AND LANGUAGES

Micronesia

This is a group of thousands of small islands in the western Pacific Ocean. Many of the islands are now small independent nations. Micronesia has a wide variety of cultures, and its people speak many different languages. The people are descended from settlers who came from other parts of the Pacific.

MINING A GREAT RESOURCE

Australia's mining industry

Australia is the second-largest gold producer in the world and the leading producer of bauxite, titanium and diamonds. The country also mines uranium, nickel, lead, zinc, tin and copper, and has its own oil fields. These natural resources are very important to the country's economy.

ABORIGINAL AUSTRALIANS

Aboriginal Australians were the first people to settle in Australia. Traditionally, they lived as hunter-gatherers, hunting and foraging food from the land. There are many different Aboriginal groups across the continent, each with its own language and traditions.

COMMON HERITAGE

Out of Africa

About 80,000 years ago, a small group of people left Africa and crossed into Arabia in search of food. All non-Africans, from Europeans to Amerindians to Aboriginal Australians, are descended from this group. Some of the people who left Africa at this time moved along the southern coast of Asia, reaching Australia about 50,000 years ago. These were the ancestors of today's Aboriginal Australian people.

CULTURE AND TRADITIONS

Body painting

Body decoration using ancestral designs is an important part of many ceremonies. Designs are painted onto the face and body using ochres (natural clays) that are ground and mixed with water.

Aboriginal culture
Boys perform a traditional dance.

Dance

Dance is an important part of Aboriginal culture. Dancing may be part of a social gathering or to mark a specific occasion, such as the opening of a new building.

Cave art

These rock paintings in Kakadu National Park represent scenes from a mythical world. The paintings are many thousands of years old.

Didgeridoo

This wind instrument is used in dance and music. A didgeridoo may be 0.8–2 metres long. The larger the instrument, the deeper its sound.

Stone mortar

A stone mortar was traditionally used to grind or crush herbs and seeds used for cooking.

Men and women

Male dancing is lively with a lot of jumping and kicking. Women have their own dances, which are less energetic and more of a loose-knee shuffle.

Homes

In the past, Aboriginal people did not build houses or huts, but lived in caves. Today, many Aborigines still live in the Australian outback, but in houses.

Boomerang

This flat, wooden weapon was traditionally used for hunting. The boomerang was thrown at its target. If it missed, the boomerang would spin round and return to the person who had thrown it.

THE SYDNEY OPERA HOUSE

One of the world's most recognizable buildings, the Sydney Opera House contains a large hall for opera, a concert hall, large and small theatres, an exhibition area and a library.

BUILDING FACT FILE

A palace of culture

The Sydney Opera House was declared a World Heritage Site by UNESCO in 2007.

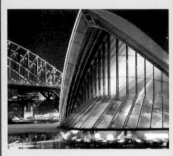

Fact file

Location:
Sydney, Australia

Kind of building:
cultural centre

Capacity (of performing spaces):
5700 spectators

Structure:
cement, pink granite and wood veneer

❶ Opera house
❷ Concert hall
❸ Restaurant

City postcard
The Sydney Opera House was opened in 1973. It cost AU$102 million to build.

Utzon Hall (opera house)

In 2004, the old hall was renamed after the Opera House's architect. The Utzon Hall is used to host a range of events, including musical performances.

Uses
The Opera House hosts
opera, ballet, concerts
and theatre in five halls.
There are also rooms
for conferences
and meetings.

Construction
The Sydney Opera
House was built in
stages between 1959
and 1973. The original
architect was Jorn
Utzon, from Denmark.

233
The number of
architects who
submitted designs
for the Opera House.

Auditorium
(concert hall)

New colonnade

The new western colonnade
opened in 2006. The new
walkway is 45 metres long.
It runs along the side of the
building, allowing light to
flood in and giving people
visiting the Opera House
views of Sydney Harbour.

The concert hall
This magnificent venue can
hold 2679 concert goers.
It is the Opera House's
largest interior venue, and
is home to the Sydney
Symphony Orchestra and
the Australian Chamber
Orchestra.

THE WORLD
IN FIGURES
INTRODUCTION

This atlas has looked at each continent in detail, examining the range of landscapes and the many different people who live in each region. The next chapter looks at the facts and figures behind many of the world's problems, from overpopulation and food sources to water shortages and energy resources. The chapter discusses how these problems affect the global economy.

FUEL
ENDLESS LINES OF FREIGHT CARRIERS FULL OF COAL ARE EXPORTED TO COUNTRIES AROUND THE WORLD TO GENERATE ELECTRICITY.

CONTINENTS AND COUNTRIES

Humankind has made all kinds of divisions and boundaries that shape the world map politically. While many of the borders have names that have existed naturally, some have been formed as a result of historical events, such as war.

BORDERS
Usually shown as lines on a map, borders mark out the geographic areas that define separate countries.

The land area

Most of the Earth's surface is covered in water. The land area, representing about one-third of the Earth, is divided into seven continents. Central America and the Caribbean is sometimes considered a subcontinent and is part of the continent of North America.

38
million

The number of times that the world's largest country, Russia, is greater than the Vatican City, the world's smallest country.

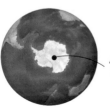

Antarctica
14,000,000 sq km

North America
24,315,410 sq km

Central America and Caribbean
758,154 sq km

Africa
30,272,922 sq km

South America
17,870,218 sq km

Africa: **53**

Central America and the Caribbean: **21**

Oceania: **14**

North America: **3**

South America: **12**

Europe: **45**

Antarctica: **0**

Asia: **48**

MANY COUNTRIES

Each flag in the illustration on the right represents a country, coloured to match the continent or subcontinent it belongs to. Antarctica is unique in having no individual countries.

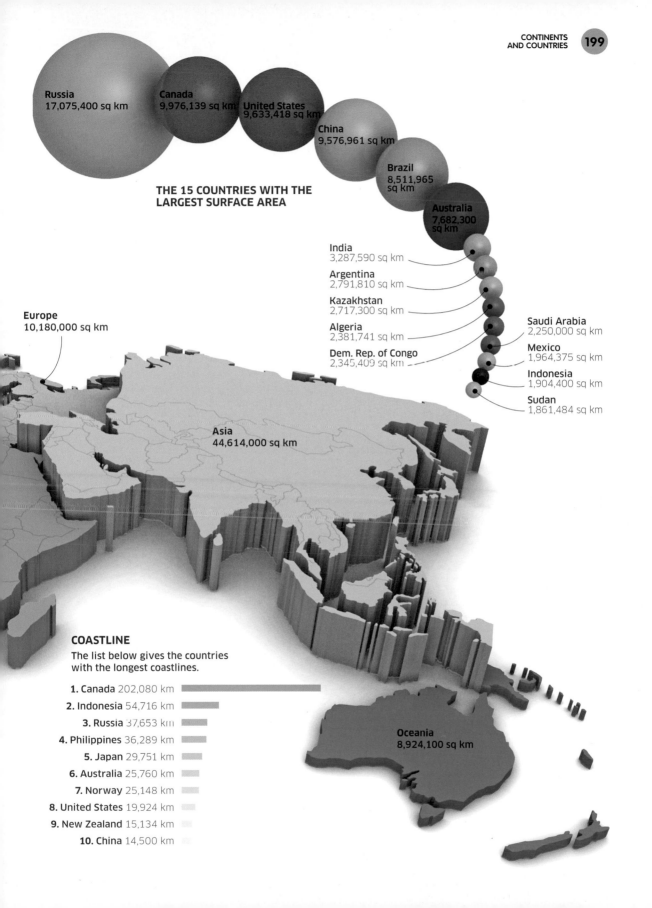

Russia
17,075,400 sq km

Canada
9,976,139 sq km

United States
9,633,418 sq km

China
9,576,961 sq km

Brazil
8,511,965
sq km

Australia
7,682,300
sq km

THE 15 COUNTRIES WITH THE LARGEST SURFACE AREA

India
3,287,590 sq km

Argentina
2,791,810 sq km

Kazakhstan
2,717,300 sq km

Algeria
2,381,741 sq km

Dem. Rep. of Congo
2,345,409 sq km

Saudi Arabia
2,250,000 sq km

Mexico
1,964,375 sq km

Indonesia
1,904,400 sq km

Sudan
1,861,484 sq km

Europe
10,180,000 sq km

Asia
44,614,000 sq km

Oceania
8,924,100 sq km

COASTLINE

The list below gives the countries with the longest coastlines.

1. Canada 202,080 km
2. Indonesia 54,716 km
3. Russia 37,653 km
4. Philippines 36,289 km
5. Japan 29,751 km
6. Australia 25,760 km
7. Norway 25,148 km
8. United States 19,924 km
9. New Zealand 15,134 km
10. China 14,500 km

CLIMATE ZONES

Different parts of the world can be divided into climate zones. These are regions where there is a similar temperature, atmospheric pressure, rainfall and other precipitation and humidity.

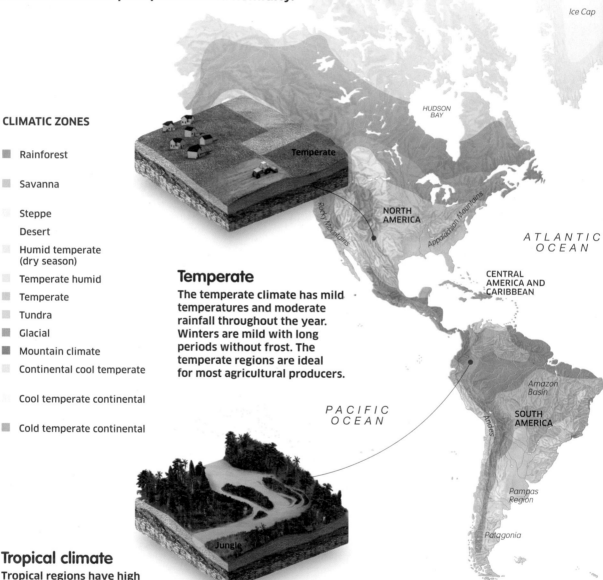

CLIMATIC ZONES

- Rainforest
- Savanna
- Steppe
- Desert
- Humid temperate (dry season)
- Temperate humid
- Temperate
- Tundra
- Glacial
- Mountain climate
- Continental cool temperate
- Cool temperate continental
- Cold temperate continental

Temperate

The temperate climate has mild temperatures and moderate rainfall throughout the year. Winters are mild with long periods without frost. The temperate regions are ideal for most agricultural producers.

Tropical climate

Tropical regions have high temperatures throughout the year, combined with heavy rains. About half of the world's population lives in tropical climates. Here, the vegetation is lush and there is a very high level of moisture caused by rainfall and plant transpiration.

Ice Cap

HUDSON BAY

NORTH AMERICA

Rocky Mountains

Appalachian Mountains

ATLANTIC OCEAN

CENTRAL AMERICA AND CARIBBEAN

PACIFIC OCEAN

Amazon Basin

SOUTH AMERICA

Andes

Pampas Region

Patagonia

Jungle

Extreme temperatures

The highest temperature was recorded in Libya in 1922: 57.8 °C. The lowest temperature was recorded in 1983 at Vostok Station, Antarctica (-89.2 °C). The area of Marble Bar in Western Australia has a constant high temperature. From 7 October 1923 to 31 April 1924, the temperature was never lower than 37.8 °C.

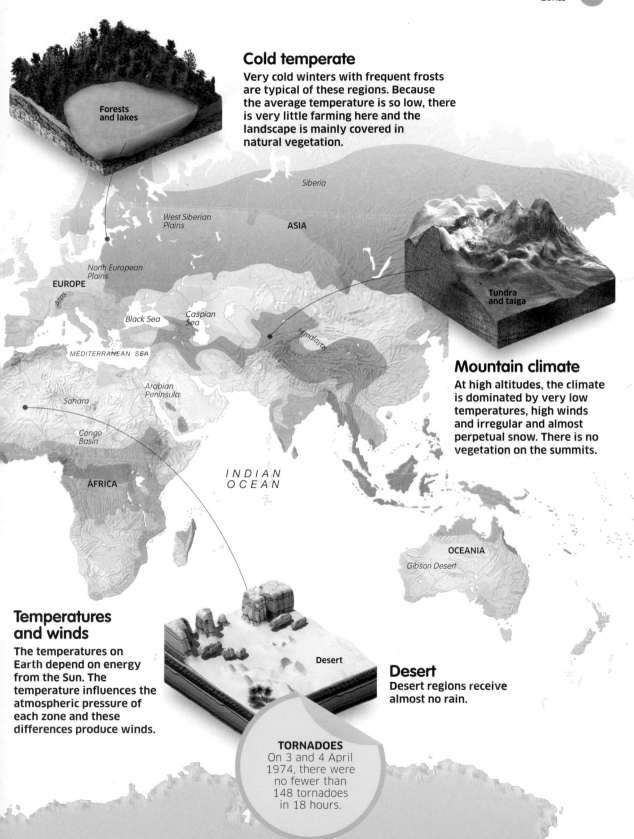

Cold temperate

Very cold winters with frequent frosts are typical of these regions. Because the average temperature is so low, there is very little farming here and the landscape is mainly covered in natural vegetation.

Forests and lakes

Siberia

West Siberian Plains

ASIA

North European Plains

EUROPE

Alps

Black Sea

Caspian Sea

MEDITERRANEAN SEA

Himalayas

Tundra and taiga

Mountain climate

At high altitudes, the climate is dominated by very low temperatures, high winds and irregular and almost perpetual snow. There is no vegetation on the summits.

Sahara

Arabian Peninsula

Congo Basin

ÁFRICA

INDIAN OCEAN

OCEANIA

Gibson Desert

Temperatures and winds

The temperatures on Earth depend on energy from the Sun. The temperature influences the atmospheric pressure of each zone and these differences produce winds.

Desert

Desert

Desert regions receive almost no rain.

TORNADOES
On 3 and 4 April 1974, there were no fewer than 148 tornadoes in 18 hours.

OVERPOPULATION

As the world population continues to increase, the pressure to meet the basic needs of life will become greater. The differences between the standard of living of the most economically developed countries and the least developed countries will remain high because the population will grow even more in poor countries.

Japan
Crowded streets
in Tokyo.

DIFFERENT VALUES

Life expectancy

This is the average number of years a person is expected to live. In Europe, during the time of the Roman Empire, the average life expectancy was 25 years. In 1900, it reached 50 across the world. Thanks to many advances in medicine, the average life expectancy now stands at 67 years. Nevertheless, there are big differences between the life expectancies of the rich and poor.

A world of difference

Life expectancy in some countries:

COUNTRY	AGE
JAPAN	82
SWITZERLAND	81
UNITED STATES	78
ARGENTINA	75
VENEZUELA	73
MONGOLIA	67
NIGERIA	47

The Future
By 2050, the United Nations predicts that the population of the Earth will be 9.1 billion people.

Asia at the head

East Asia has the highest concentration of people in the world.

Overcrowding

With nearly 17 million people in Calcutta, India, problems such as poverty, water pollution, traffic and noise are common.

Solutions

Solutions to problems such as food, water and energy shortages – and also poor healthcare and education – need to be found to support the ever-growing global population.

COUNTRIES WITH MOST PEOPLE

Two-thirds of the world population live in just 16 countries.

3.5% Indonesia

4.5% United States of America

18% India

19% China

55% Rest of the world

URBAN GEOGRAPHY

Huge city

A conurbation is the result of growth and expansion of a central city. Neighbouring towns or cities that have developed are absorbed to form a single unit.

CONURBATIONS	PEOPLE
Tokyo, Japan	38,000,000
Guangzhou, China	24,500,000
Seoul, South Korea	24,200,000
Mexico City, Mexico	23,400,000
New Delhi, India	23,200,000

AGRICULTURE

The production of genetically modified (GM) crops is increasing. Scientists believe that genetic modification can improve crops, and reduce costs and the amount of chemicals used. Some environmentalists warn that not enough is known about the effect of GM crops on the environment and on consumers.

NO LIMITS
The production of GM crops has affected both industrialized and developing countries.

Countries with GM crops

This map shows the distribution of GM crops in 2010, in millions of hectares (ha).

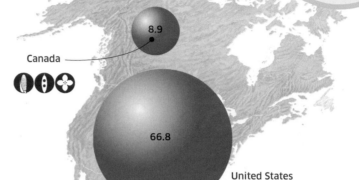

Canada 8.9

France 0.05

Spain 0.1

Portugal 0.

United States 66.8

Mexico 0.1

Honduras 0.05

ATLANTIC OCEAN

Colombia 0.05

Brazil 25.5

Bolivia 0.9

Paraguay 2.6

Chile 0.05

Uruguay 1.1

PACIFIC OCEAN

Argentina 23

PERCENTAGE OF FARMED LAND IN ARGENTINA

54% GM crops (soya, maize and cotton)

46% Natural crops

NATURAL AND GM SOYA AND COTTON CROPS AROUND THE WORLD

Soya

24% Natural

76% GM

Cotton

62% GM

38% Natural

90

The percentage of all GM crops produced in Argentina, Brazil, the United States and Canada.

TOP PRODUCERS OF WHEAT
In millions of tonnes per year

1. China 112
2. India 79
3. USA 68
4. Russia 64
5. France 39
6. Canada 29
7. Germany 26
8. Ukraine 26
9. Australia 21
10. Pakistan 21

TOP PRODUCERS OF POTATOES
In millions of tonnes per year

1. China 72
2. Russia 36
3. India 26
4. USA 20
5. Ukraine 19
6. Poland 11
7. Germany 11
8. Belarus 8
9. Netherlands 7
10. France 6

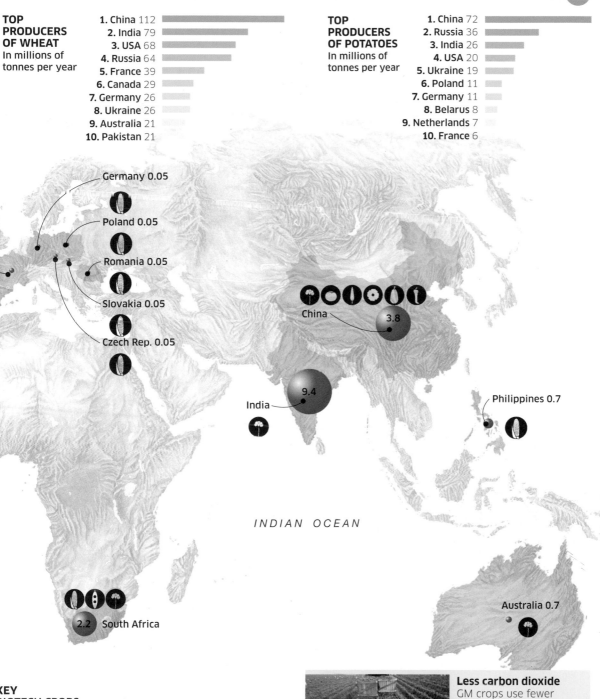

Germany 0.05

Poland 0.05

Romania 0.05

Slovakia 0.05

Czech Rep. 0.05

China

3.8

India

9.4

Philippines 0.7

INDIAN OCEAN

2.2 South Africa

Australia 0.7

KEY BIOTECH CROPS

 Corn
 Carnation
 Rape
 Tomato
 Soya
 Cotton

 Poplar
 Petunia
 Alfalfa
 Pumpkin
Papaya
Pepper

Less carbon dioxide
GM crops use fewer chemicals and so emit less carbon dioxide. Reducing carbon dioxide (a greenhouse gas) in the atmosphere means that the greenhouse effect has less impact.

FISHING

In its global report on fishing, the Food and Agriculture Organization of the United Nations (FAO) stated that 19 per cent of fishing resources are overexploited and 8 per cent are depleted. Although the situation has remained stable since 2000, overfishing will ultimately have a serious impact on the world's food supply.

All at sea

The seas and oceans provide 90 per cent of fish that is caught. The remaining 10 per cent come from fresh water sources. The environmental charity Greenpeace has called for a law to protect 40 per cent of the oceans from overfishing.

Hungry oceans

Due to the overfishing of anchovy and mackerel, natural predators of these fish are left with a decreasing source of food. This has affected both dolphins and tuna.

Shrimp farming

The world shrimp production has stabilized as a result of shrimp farming. India, China, the United States, Thailand, Indonesia, Mexico, Malaysia, Japan, Vietnam and Brazil are the leading countries engaged in shrimp farming.

MAJOR EXPORTERS (2008)

These are the annual figures of the top fish-exporting countries, in billions of dollars.

1. China 10.1
2. Norway 6.9
3. Thailand 6.5
4. Denmark 4.6
5. Vietnam 4.5
6. USA 4.5

Work

Fishing is very important to the livelihoods of millions of people around the world. More than 60 million people are said to work in the fishing industry, and half of this workforce are women

SOURCE OF PROTEIN

Important values

Fish and fish products make up 15 per cent of the animal protein eaten by half of the global population. This means that on average, each person eats about 17 kilograms of fish each year.

LIVESTOCK

Livestock is an important resource and a good indicator of
the economy of a country. It is is used for meat and other
products, such as leather and wool. In less economically
developed countries, animals are also used to move
agricultural equipment and as a means of transport.

DEFORESTATION
Around 80 per cent
of the Brazilian
Amazon Rainforest
has been deforested
to raise cattle.

PROTECTION
HEALTH

Health problems

According to the FAO, the risk of
disease being transmitted from
animals to humans has increased
because more animals are being
reared. Influenza A is one
such disease.

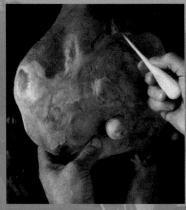

Meat producers

There are about 1300 million cattle
in the world. Countries such as
the United States, Brazil and China
have large areas of fertile land for
raising cattle.

Dairy producers

The graph below shows the major
dairy producers. Consumption
of dairy products varies widely
around the world. It depends on
the eating habits and diet of the
population as well as its wealth.

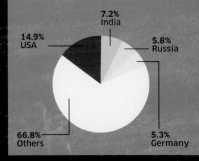

14.9%
USA

7.2%
India

5.8%
Russia

66.8%
Others

5.3%
Germany

Poultry

According to the FAO, in the last decade, the consumption of poultry products in less economically developed countries increased each year by 5.8 per cent.

POULTRY PRODUCTION (in thousands of tonnes)

1. USA 19,691
2. China 15,052
3. Brazil 9225
4. Mexico 2585
5. India 2313

Meat production

As the global population grows, there is an increase in the demand for meat products in less economically developed countries. The FAO reports that meat production will grow from 278 million tonnes a year to 463 million tonnes by 2050.

CHANGING STATISTICS

World meat consumption

The protein intake from eating meat has changed over time. In 1968, the global average of proteins from meat per person per day was 9.2 grams. In 1998, this had increased to 12.6 grams.

MEATS CONSUMED

Pork 40%

Poultry 29%

Beef 26%

Lamb 5%

PER PERSON PER DAY

PLACE	GRAMS
Developed countries	224
Latin America	147
Far East and South Asia	112
Middle East	54
Developing countries	47
Africa	31

A THIRSTY WORLD

According to the World Health Organization, about 900 million people worldwide lack access to safe drinking water. Another 2.5 billion, over a third of the world's population, lack adequate sanitation systems. In some countries, water is so scarce that not a drop is wasted: the water used to wash a baby is then used for washing clothes or cleaning the kitchen.

RIGHTS
Environmental organizations believe that water is not a commodity but a basic human right.

Human water consumption

This map shows that the water intended for human consumption is much less than that used in agriculture and industry.

MAJOR CONSUMERS OF WATER

- Industrial use
- Industrial and agricultural use
- Industrial use, with important domestic use
- Domestic use
- Domestic and agricultural use
- Agricultural use, but with important domestic use
- Agricultural use
- Agricultural use, with important industrial use
- Agricultural use, with less important industrial use
- No data

Water shortages

In many African countries people have to queue each day to get water. Every year 1.5 million children die from diarrhoea and dehydration that could have been prevented by having access to clean drinking water.

Human health

It is estimated that to ensure a person's basic needs, such as washing, sanitation, drinking and cooking, each person needs 20 to 50 litres of clean, uncontaminated water each day.

13

The percentage of people living in Afghanistan who have access to safe drinking water.

Role of women

Women play a key role in domestic water use because they are often responsible for cooking, looking after children, washing dishes, clothes and the house. In places where there is no running water, it is often the women in the area who walk to fetch water. However, women are often left out of decisions on the planning and management of water resources.

OIL

The world's richest countries depend on oil as their main source of energy. However, we know that oil reserves are running out. As a result, the price of oil has gone up and this has affected the global economy.

LESS OIL
Supplies of oil and natural gas (also found in oil fields) are going to become smaller over the next decade.

Map of oil consumption and production

This map shows the largest users and producers of oil. In red is the amount used each day, while blue shows the amount produced each day. The figures are the amount used or produced per day in millions of barrels (one barrel is equivalent to 159 litres of oil).

⬤ **The biggest users**
The world uses about 85 million barrels of oil every day. The biggest user is the United States.

⬤ **The biggest producers**
Saudi Arabia, Russia and the United States are the biggest oil producers.

▪ **Main shipping routes**
▪ **Alternative shipping routes**

Canada
2264   3288

USA
20,687

8330

Mexico
1997 3707

ATLANTIC OCEAN

PACIFIC OCEAN

Venezuela
2803

Brazil
2217

70
The percentage of oil consumed in the United States that is used as fuel for transport.

USES OF OIL

Fuel
About 95 per cent of the world's vehicles use fuels made from oil. As a result, the cost of transporting goods goes up when the price of oil goes up.

Making electricity
Much of the world's electricity is made in power stations using oil or gas as fuel. These power stations need to be replaced with power stations that use other sources of energy.

Rising oil prices

Possible causes for the rise in the price of oil:
1. There has been a rise in demand for oil in growing economies, such as India and China.

2. The amount of oil left in current oilfields is falling, and those who consume the oil have as yet to find a new source.

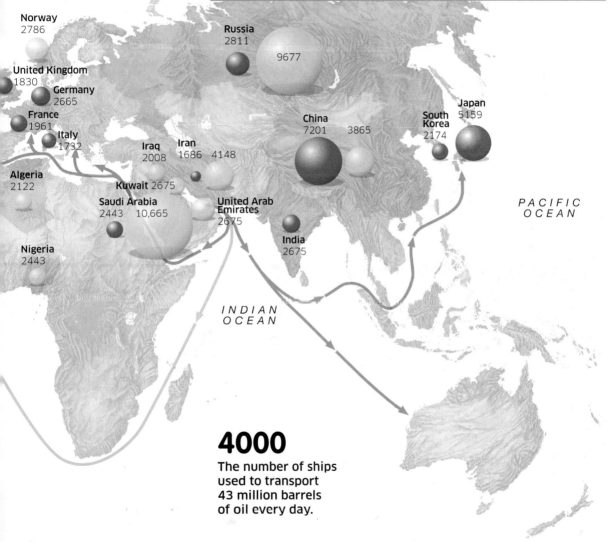

Norway
2786

Russia
2811

9677

United Kingdom
1830

Germany
2665

France
1961

Italy
1732

China
7201   3865

South Korea
2174

Japan
5159

Iraq
2008

Iran
1686   4148

Algeria
2122

Kuwait 2675

Saudi Arabia
2443   10,665

United Arab Emirates
2675

India
2675

Nigeria
2443

PACIFIC OCEAN

INDIAN OCEAN

4000
The number of ships used to transport 43 million barrels of oil every day.

Plastics

Many goods are made of plastic, which is a material made partly from oil. Scientists are now looking for other materials to use instead of plastics.

Other uses

Oil is used to make many things, including dyes, fertilizer and asphalt (left, used in building roads). An increase in the price of oil affects a huge number of the things that we use.

LIGHTING THE PLANET

Seen from space, the Earth is well lit by electricity. The generation of electricity by burning fossil fuels (coal, oil and gas) has serious environmental implications. As a result, new technologies are being tested and alternative sources of energy are being sought.

NO STARS
In many cities, stars cannot be seen in the night sky due to the reflection of electric lights.

Planet of night light

At nightfall, in many urban settings, the sunlight is replaced by electrical lighting until the Sun rises again.

London, UK

París, France

Madrid, Spain

New York, USA

Los Angeles, USA

Miami, USA

Caracas, Venezuela

CREATING ELECTRICITY

Electricity has to be generated. To do this, different sources are used. Most of these sources, such as coal, oil and gas, cause high levels of pollution and/or increased carbon dioxide (CO_2) emissions.

Oil (5.8%)
Accounts for 38 per cent of CO_2 emissions into the atmosphere.

Other (2.3%)
These are clean and renewable energies, such as solar, wind, geothermal and biomass.

Nuclear (14.8%)
Clean and virtually renewable but has the problem of radioactive waste and possible accidents.

Coal (41%)
The most polluting of all power sources and is responsible for 42 per cent of the CO_2 emissions into the atmosphere.

Río de Janeiro, Brazil
Sao Paulo, Brazil

Buenos Aires, Argentina

Hydroelectric (16%)
It is clean and renewable but damming rivers causes ecological problems and displacement of humans.

Gas (20.1%)
It accounts for 19 per cent of CO_2 emissions into the atmosphere.

65
The percentage of humans who live under electrically lit skies.

Light pollution

Electric lighting has been one of the most remarkable human inventions. However, electric lights also cause massive pollution.

Correct   Incorrect

Increasing

This drawing shows how artificial lighting can be used effectively to reduce light pollution.

Moscow, Russia

Beijing, China

Rome, Italy

Tokyo, Japan

Seoul, South Korea

Taipei, Taiwan

Mumbai, India

Hong Kong, China

Bangkok, Thailand

New Delhi, India

Johannesburg, South Africa

Sydney, Australia

MAJOR PRODUCERS

The terawatt per hour (TWh) is used to measure large amounts of electrical energy and is equivalent to one billion watts.

1. USA 22.6%
2. China 15.2%
3. Japan 5.8%
4. Russia 5.3%
5. India 3.9%
6. Germany 3.3%
7. Canada 3.2%
8. France 3%
9. Brazil 2.2%
10. South Korea 2.1%

The United States consumes nearly one-third of the world production of electricity from nuclear sources. France and Japan are major producers of this type of energy.

MAKING CONNECTIONS

According to recent research, one in four people on Earth use the internet. This new reality has accelerated to unprecedented levels the process of globalization that is facing our world.

FACEBOOK
In 2010, according to IWS (see below), the total number of Facebook users was estimated to be 517,760,460.

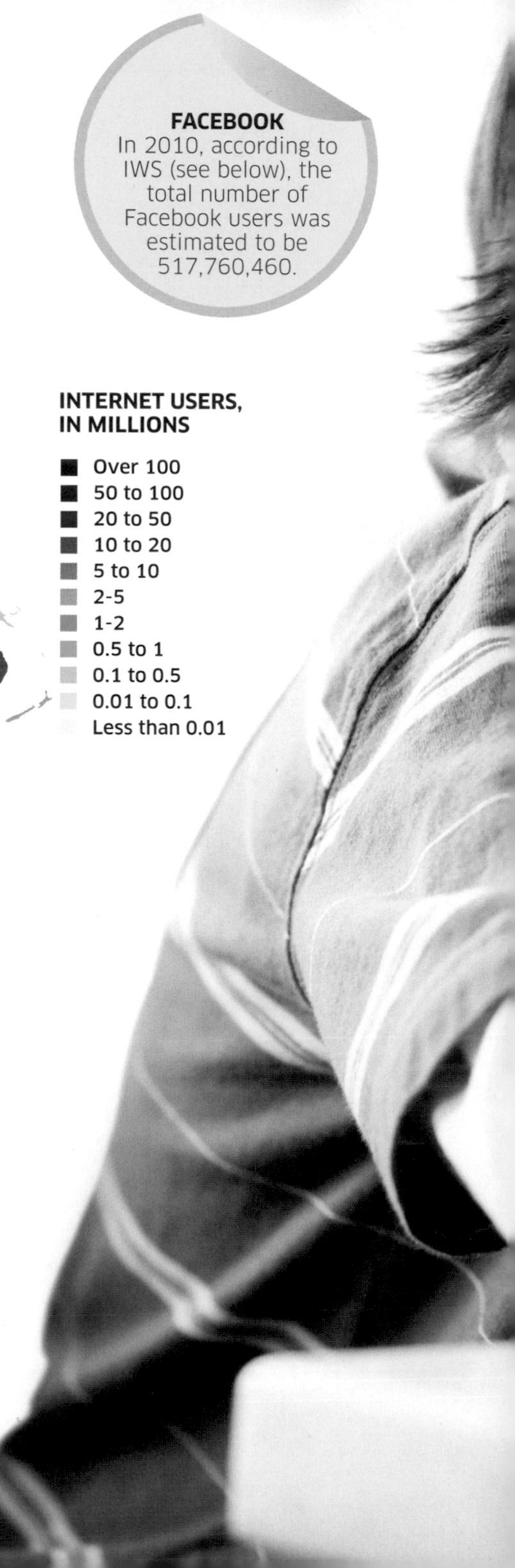

Radiography of the network

On average, 32 per cent of the world's population has internet access. However, this is not uniform and the most populous countries, with a certain level of development, have the highest access.

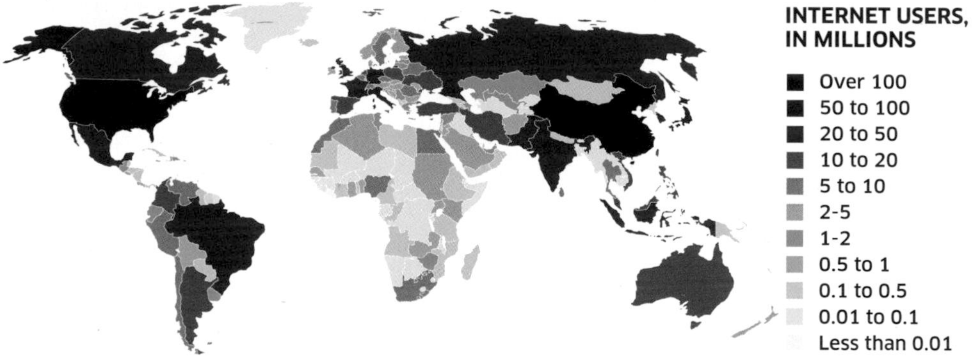

INTERNET USERS, IN MILLIONS
Over 100
50 to 100
20 to 50
10 to 20
5 to 10
2-5
1-2
0.5 to 1
0.1 to 0.5
0.01 to 0.1
Less than 0.01

OF 1000 INTERNET USERS...

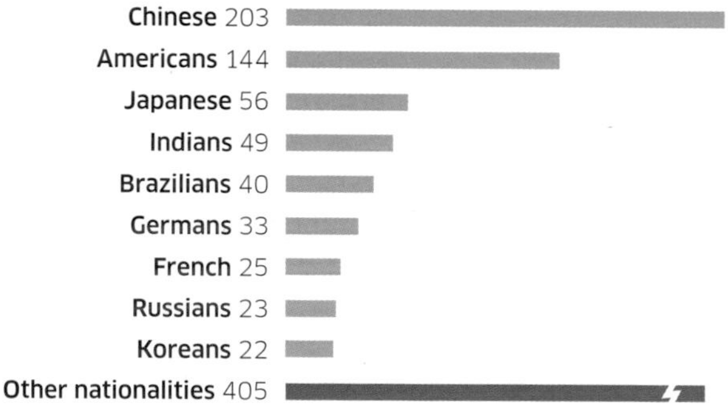

Chinese 203
Americans 144
Japanese 56
Indians 49
Brazilians 40
Germans 33
French 25
Russians 23
Koreans 22
Other nationalities 405

2011

According to Internet World Stats (IWS), there were over 2000 million internet users.

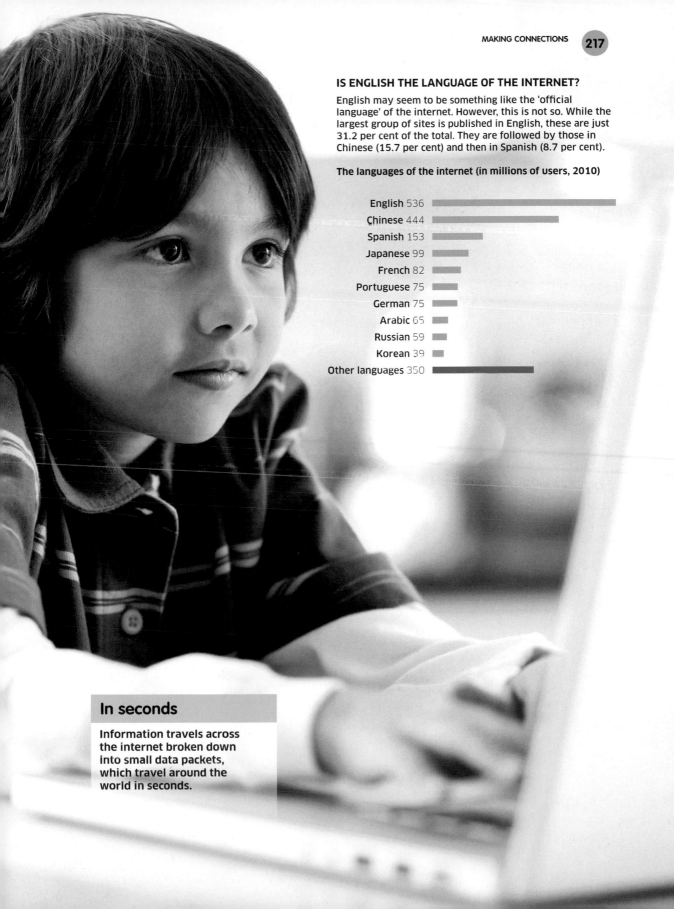

IS ENGLISH THE LANGUAGE OF THE INTERNET?

English may seem to be something like the 'official language' of the internet. However, this is not so. While the largest group of sites is published in English, these are just 31.2 per cent of the total. They are followed by those in Chinese (15.7 per cent) and then in Spanish (8.7 per cent).

The languages of the internet (in millions of users, 2010)

English	536
Chinese	444
Spanish	153
Japanese	99
French	82
Portuguese	75
German	75
Arabic	65
Russian	59
Korean	39
Other languages	350

In seconds

Information travels across the internet broken down into small data packets, which travel around the world in seconds.

GLOSSARY

ACOUSTICS
The properties or qualities of a room or building that determine how sound is transmitted in it.

ADAPTATIONS
Changes to animals and plants over a long period of time to ensure their survival in a specific biome. For example, animals found at the Poles usually have very thick coats.

AMPHITHEATRE
An open, circular or oval building, with levels of seating around a central space, used for events such as drama or sports.

ANCESTORS
People from whom another person is descended.

ANIMISM
A religious belief that everything on Earth is imbued with a spirit.

ANTHROPOLOGISTS
People who study and compare human societies and cultures.

ASTRONOMICAL CLOCK
A clock that shows the positions of the Sun, Moon, planets and large constellations of stars.

AVALANCHES
Large bodies of snow, ice and rocks falling rapidly down a mountainside.

BAUXITE
A clayey rock from which aluminium is mined.

BIODIVERSITY
The variety of plant and animal life in a particular place.

CARBON DIOXIDE
A colourless gas found in the atmosphere, which is given off when humans breathe out.

CARGO
Goods carried on a ship, aircraft or in a motor vehicle.

CARNIVOROUS
Describes animals that eat only meat.

CONTINENTAL DRIFT
The gradual movement of the continents across the Earth's surface.

CONURBATION
A large urban area in which several towns merge with the suburbs of a central city.

COSMOPOLITAN
Describes something, such as a city, with many different people and cultures.

CREMATE
To burn a dead person's body.

DEHYDRATION
When the body loses a lot of water. Dehydration can cause a dry, sticky mouth, sleepiness, and can lead to vomiting and death.

ELEVATION
The height of a mountain.

EROSION
The gradual wearing away of something by water, wind or ice.

EUROPEAN UNION (EU)
An economic and political union of 27 countries within Europe.

EXPEDITION
A journey undertaken by a team or group of people to discover and explore a new place.

EXTINCT
Describes a plant or animal that no longer survives. For example, the Arctic reindeer is extinct.

FAUNA
Animals.

FERTILE
Land of a quality on which crops can be grown.

FLORA
Plants.

FOLD MOUNTAINS
Mountains that are formed when two tectonic plates are pushed together.

FOSSIL
Describes something that has become preserved in rock, or fossilized.

GENETICALLY MODIFIED
Describes something that has been changed by scientists to produce certain characteristics. For example, animals can be injected with hormones to produce more meat.

GLACIER
A slowly moving mass or river of ice.

HEATWAVE
Abnormally hot weather for a long period of time.

HERBIVORES
Animals, such as elephants and giraffes, that eat only plants.

HIV
Short for the human immunodeficiency virus. This is the virus that causes AIDS, an illness that can be fatal.

HUNTER-GATHERER
A person who lives by hunting, fishing and harvesting wild food.

ICE CAP
A covering of ice over a large area, usually at the Poles.

ICEBERG
A large floating piece of ice that has been carried out to sea.

IMMIGRANTS
People from a different country.

IMPORT
To bring goods into a country.

INDUSTRIALIZE
To develop industries on a large scale.

INSCRIPTIONS
Something 'written' on a monument.

LAVA
Hot molten or semi-fluid rock that has erupted from a volcano.

LIMESTONE
A hard rock used in building.

LUNAR CALENDAR
A calendar based on the phases of the Moon.

MARSUPIAL
A mammal, usually found in Australia, whose young are carried in a pouch on the mother's belly.

MAUSOLEUM
A large building that houses a tomb or several tombs.

MIGRATE
To move from one country or region to another.

MUDSLIDES
A mass of mud that has fallen down a hillside or other slope.

NICKEL
A silvery-white metal.

NOCTURNAL
Describes animals, such as owls, that are active mainly at night.

NOMADIC
Describes people that travel from place to place.

NUCLEAR POWER
Electricity generated from a nuclear reactor.

OTTOMAN EMPIRE
A Turkish empire that lasted from the end of the 13th century to the beginning of the 20th century.

OUTBACK
The inland areas of Australia where very few people live.

OZONE LAYER
A layer of gases around the Earth that absorbs most of the radiation reaching the Earth from the Sun.

PADDIES
Fields where rice is grown.

PAPYRUS
A water plant used in ancient Egypt to make paper.

PERMAFROST
A thick layer of soil that remains frozen throughout the year.

PHARAOH
A ruler of ancient Egypt.

PLATEAU
A flat area of land that is usually at a high altitude.

PLATINUM
A precious silvery-white metal.

POLYTHEISM
The belief in or worship of more than one god.

RENAISSANCE
The growth of European art and literature from the 14th to the 16th century.

RENEWABLE ENERGY
Energy from a source that will not run out, such as the Sun.

SARCOPHAGUS
A stone coffin.

SCANDINAVIAN
Describes someone or something from Scandinavia (Norway, Sweden and Denmark).

SCAVENGERS
Animals, such as hyenas, that feed on dead animals, plant material or rubbish.

SOLAR POWER
Electricity generated by harnessing the Sun's energy.

SYMMETRICAL
Describes something made up of exactly the same parts facing each other.

TECTONIC PLATES
Pieces of the Earth's crust and upper mantle.

TERRACED GARDEN
A garden that has steps or raised areas.

TITANIUM
A hard silver-grey metal.

TRIBUTARY
A river or stream flowing into a larger river or lake.

TROPICAL STORM
A storm that has thunderstorms, very strong winds and brings with it heavy rain.

URANIUM
A silvery-white metal, used to create nuclear power.

URBANIZATION
The process whereby a place becomes more urban or city-like.

VIADUCT
A bridge made up of several small spans.

INDEX